DATE DUE

WITH THE

CUSTOMER
FROM HELL

DEALING
WITH THE
CUSTOMER
FROM HELL

A Survival Guide

Shaun Belding

Stoddart

Published in 2000 by Stoddart Publishing Co. Limited
34 Lesmill Road, Toronto, Canada M3B 2T6
180 Varick Street, 9th Floor, New York, New York 10014

Distributed in Canada by:
General Distribution Services Ltd.
325 Humber College Blvd., Toronto, Ontario M9W 7C3
Tel. (416) 213-1919   Fax (416) 213-1917
Email cservice@genpub.com

Distributed in the United States by:
General Distribution Services Inc.
4500 Witmer Industrial Estates, Niagara Falls, New York 14305-1386
Toll-free Tel. 1-800-805-1083   Toll-free Fax 1-800-481-6207
Email gdsinc@genpub.com

04   03   02   01   00   1   2   3   4   5

Canadian Cataloguing in Publication Data

Belding, Shaun
Dealing with the customer from hell: a survival guide

ISBN 0-7737-6103-9

1. Customer relations. I. Title.

HF5415.5.B442 2000   658.8'12   C00-930022-8

U.S. Cataloging-in-Publication Data
(Library of Congress Standards)

Belding, Shaun, 1957–
Dealing with the customer from hell: a survival guide/Shaun Belding.
— 1st ed.
[192]p. : ill. ; cm.
Summary: Realistic, practical solutions to dealing with difficult customers
through LESTER, a six-step guide to solving difficult situations.
ISBN 0-7737-6103-9 (pbk.)
1. Customer services. 2. Management. I. Title.
658.8/ 12 21   2000   CIP

Cover design: Angel Guerra
Text design: Tannice Goddard

THE CANADA COUNCIL | LE CONSEIL DES ARTS
FOR THE ARTS | DU CANADA
SINCE 1957 | DEPUIS 1957

*We acknowledge for their financial support of our
publishing program the Canada Council, the Ontario Arts
Council, and the Government of Canada through the
Book Publishing Industry Development Program (BPIDP).*

Printed and bound in Canada

This book is dedicated to:

*Mom, for teaching me the value of laughter
(and of brushing after meals);
Margo, Lee, and Jackie, for filling my life with joy;
Yvette, for filling it with love.*

～❧

*Shari, Brian, and Bridget, for the words and the wisdom;
Bob and Linda, for being so darned wonderful.*

Contents

Introduction: To Hell and Back Again

*"What a lovely day. You know,
if I do nothing else today,
I think I'm going to make some
poor salesperson's life miserable."*

The Customer from Hell. The favourite topic of retail people everywhere. Reports of this notorious monster can be heard daily in store lunchrooms and mall food courts across the country. The air is filled with outrageous, absurd, and sometimes terrifying tales of a barely human, impossible customer who preys indiscriminately on unsuspecting retail salespeople. Like emotional vampires, these customers drain us of all positive energy and replace it with feelings of frustration, anger, and hurt.

You do know who I mean, don't you? These are the monstrous customers whom you imagine wake up in the morning, stretch, look out the window, and say to themselves, "What a lovely day. You know, if I do nothing else today, I think I'm going to make some poor salesperson's life miserable." Then they sit there and, over their breakfasts of cold gruel, carefully plan their strategies for systematically ruining your day.

But who are these people? What are they really thinking? Why do they do the things they do? Why do they seem to have such a profound impact on our lives? More important, what can we do about them?

I've had the great pleasure of meeting and working with thousands of retail people in the past few years, and of the hundreds of seminars I've conducted I don't think one has gone by without at least someone asking, "How do you handle difficult customers?"

Not long ago, a young woman who worked as a part-time salesperson for a national stationery chain recounted to me in painful detail a truly horrendous customer-contact experience. A man had come up to her, incensed that the store didn't have adequate wheelchair access. He cursed at her. He shouted at the top of his lungs. Nothing she said to the man seemed to help.

How vivid was her memory of this man? Well, she was able to describe to me exactly what he looked like. She remembered the clothes he was wearing. She remembered what his voice sounded like. She even remembered the scent of his cologne. She was able to reproduce their conversation word for word.

As she told me her story, her voice became increasingly strained and her shoulders began to slump. I listened and watched with fascination as she relived the emotions of the moment. This customer had become real to her again, surfacing to spoil yet another day. She was visibly shaken.

What I found most disturbing was that the unpleasant scene she was recounting had happened more than six months earlier. How many thousands of customers had she seen in the meantime? How many thousands of positive customer experiences had she had over those six months? Yet this one awful experience had stuck with her like a wad of gum to a shoe, affecting both her personal motivation and her day-to-day performance.

I suspect that anyone who has worked in retail for more than a month has had at least one of these encounters and has experienced the same kind of trauma. Some of the stories I've heard would curl the toes of the most grizzled of veterans. To be honest, as much as I hate to admit it, there was a time when I made light of these kinds of stories and the impact that Customers from Hell can have on our emotional well-being. "These people represent probably less than one-tenth of one percent of the people who shop in our stores," I thought knowingly. "Aren't we better off concentrating on the 99.9 percent of our customers who are pleasant to deal with?"

I have since come to realize that while it is true that Customers from Hell represent just a very small fraction of the customers who come into a store, it is equally true that this small group profoundly affects how we feel about ourselves and how we interact with our other customers.

Customers from Hell can be broken down into two basic categories: unsatisfied and unreasonable. An unsatisfied customer is one who had either positive expectations that were not met or negative expectations that were met. An unreasonable customer is one with unreasonable expectations — either unreasonable expectations of you or unreasonable expectations of what is acceptable in their own behaviour.

When these expectations are met — or not met, as the case may be — and conflict arises, our unsatisfied and unreasonable customers can exhibit a wide range of behaviours that most of us find unsettling at best. These behaviours can include belligerence, swearing, lying, negotiation, verbal abusiveness, whining, impatience, shouting, demands on your time, condescension, and other equally pleasant things.

Most Customers from Hell appear, at first glance, to be acting unreasonably. What we will discover as we explore the actions of these customers, however, is that unreasonable and inappropriate behaviour does not necessarily mean unreasonable expectations or an unreasonable person. Most often, what you as the retailer are experiencing is an unsatisfied customer behaving in an inappropriate manner.

You see, most Customers from Hell are no different than you or me. They don't belong to some evil Customer from Hell cult, and they're not really going out of their way to get you. Basically, they're pretty decent people whom you've just been privileged to catch at their worst. Can you honestly say you've never said or done things you've regretted later? Who is the Customer from Hell? Look into the mirror the next time you're having a bad day. What are they really thinking? They probably think they are the victims, not you.

But why do Customers from Hell affect us so dramatically? Well, for starters, retail is an exceptionally stressful occupation. If you work full time in an average store, you're going to come face to face with some 20,000 to 50,000 customers every single year. If you are part time, you'll come in contact with maybe half that many. Those are big numbers, and it is an awful lot of humanity for anybody to have to cope with. It's not hard to understand how someone seemingly intent on adding unexpected stress to people's lives could push some of us right off the deep end.

Basic psychology also plays a large part. Our actions and emotional states are dictated largely by what we focus on. If we focus on the positive things in our lives, we tend to be happy. If we focus on the negative, we tend to be unhappy. This is somewhat of a simplification, of course, but it is nonetheless true. What works against us is that we have a tendency to focus more on the negative than on the positive. Our attention is drawn to the exceptions, not to the rules.

If you don't believe me, try this experiment just for fun. Some evening, corral someone — a friend, a spouse — and ask that person to list five things that went wrong that day. Five negative things. Five things that could have gone a little better. Within a minute or two, you will have your list, and it will likely not be restricted to just five items. Then ask the same person to list five things that went right that day. Five good, positive things that happened. Notice how much longer the second list takes to complete — if it ever gets completed at all.

The media have known about and exploited this quirk of human nature for years. Dozens of newspapers have attempted to develop a "good news" format, only to have it quickly perish. Human nature. Go figure. It's no surprise, then, that our own personal traumas stick with us for a very long time.

Now, I'm not suggesting for a moment that we are negative by nature. It's just that negative events seem to be that much more memorable to us. Why is that? Why are Customers from Hell so memorable? Why do we experience that gnawing, gut-chewing anxiety when we encounter them? Why are these situations so darned stressful?

The answer is experience, or perhaps the lack of experience. Most of us have never before had a real need, or an opportunity, to learn skills for coping positively with people who behave badly. Think about it for a moment. When you were growing up, didn't your parents spend most of their time teaching you concepts like sharing, respect, love, and caring, among other things? In school, didn't your teachers work on concepts of teamwork and responsibility? At work, aren't you told to smile and sell? For the most part, we are taught how to interact positively.

We usually learn how to deal with conflict, however, by trial and error, and as a result, our solutions are rarely productive. Some of us have learned to strike back, to flee, or to sulk. Some of us cope by crying, shouting, or snapping back. The truth is that most of us have never learned the skill of resolving conflict in a positive manner. In fact, most of us just don't experience conflict frequently enough to practise coping with it positively.

We're also not used to negotiating from the position of underdog — unless you happen to have been one of those kids who was the playground bully's favourite target. Like the bully, the Customer from Hell typically has an agenda that is different from our own. His goal most often is to "win" — either emotionally or substantively. Our goal is customer satisfaction, which can be a very tough pill to swallow when the "satisfaction" sought by the Customer from Hell appears outrageous and unreasonable.

You can't win with a Customer from Hell — it's not possible. Of course, you certainly don't want to lose, either. Fortunately, it is possible, in most cases, to resolve a situation to everyone's satisfaction. The answer is much simpler than you may think. Not easy, mind you, but simple. You really just need to fine-tune and focus your active listening skills, and develop proactive, positive language skills.

In *Dealing with the Customer from Hell,* I will be talking about some proven methods for managing difficult situations and difficult customers. But before we get into the good stuff, perhaps I should clarify what this book is not. Unlike many other strategies, this is not a personality-based approach to conflict resolution. Many of the techniques presented in other books and programs focus on various personalities or behaviours exhibited by the people with whom you are in conflict, and offer methods for responding to each personality type. These techniques outline various forms of behaviour, such as aggressive behaviour, passive behaviour, passive/aggressive behaviour, and so on.

Personality, of course, does play a role in conflict. As a result, a fundamental understanding of people and their personalities is unquestionably important. An understanding of personalities is particularly relevant with "environmental" conflict (i.e., coping with a co-worker). But I believe that in situational conflict, such as with customers, personality is only one of many elements of which we need to be aware. More important, I'm not convinced that when conflict with a customer arises, many of us have the ability, in the heat of "battle," to instantly analyze the other person's behaviour and respond appropriately and constructively.

The skills and tips outlined in the book are not restricted for use with difficult customers or in difficult situations. What I will be covering are powerful communication skills that have a wide range of applications beyond conflict management. This book concentrates on a universal six-step procedure that, when executed properly, will help you resolve the vast majority of difficult situations in which you are likely to find yourself. Each of the steps individually introduces skills that apply equally to family, friendship, and business relationships.

The book also explores and offers solutions for specific situations that cannot be resolved using the six-step process. But I think you will find that these situations and the customers they involve are, thankfully, few and far between.

Finally, remember that you need to actively practise and rehearse the techniques, and take a painfully honest look at any of your own idiosyncrasies that contribute to conflict. The stuff in here works, I can promise that. How well it works depends on the depth of your commitment to changing your approach to conflict.

Hell Is Paved with Good Intentions

Here must all distrust be left behind;
all cowardice must be ended.

— *DANTE'S* INFERNO

······

One

Customers and Their Expectations

··

*The essence of resolving conflict is to first separate
the expectations that lead to conflict
from the behaviour that fuels it, and then to
work to understand those expectations.*

··

Have you ever noticed that Customers from Hell seem to appear out of nowhere? One minute you're merrily stocking the shelves and the next you have some lunatic screaming in your face. Have you ever asked yourself, "What is her problem?" or "What has got into him?" or "Why does she act that way?" Sure you have.

Unfortunately, we tend to ask these questions *after* the customers have left the store. If we took the time to find the answers while the customers were still around, we would

resolve many of these conflicts with a lot less headache —
and maybe even make a sale. The answers to these questions
tell us a lot about why our Customers from Hell behave
the way they do — what they expect and what has created
these expectations. And as you'll discover, an understanding
of expectations plays a huge role in how well we respond to
these situations.

All customers who come in your door bring with them
a set of expectations. These expectations are created by
their needs, circumstances, past experiences, personalities,
and personal situations. Most have positive expectations, but
some have negative and even unreasonable ones. With the
majority of customers, these expectations do not create any
particular challenges for us. Occasionally, however, they will
have a significant effect on a customer's behaviour.

Let's take a look at some of the positive, negative, and
unreasonable expectations customers may have.

Positive expectations include:

1. They believe you have what they need.
2. They think you will be able to solve a problem.
3. They believe you will care.
4. They believe you will be professional.
5. They believe your products or services will be reliable.
6. They believe you will be trustworthy.
7. They believe their business is valuable to you.
8. They expect you to be cheerful.
9. They expect your prices to be fair.
10. They expect you to stand behind your products or
    services.

Negative expectations include:

1. They believe you will be unskilled.
2. They expect to get a hassle when they have a problem.
3. They believe you do not care.
4. They expect you not to have enough authority to handle a situation.
5. They think you're going to try to take advantage of them.
6. They believe your product is of poor quality.
7. They think your product is overpriced.
8. They believe you're interested only in a quick commission sale.
9. They expect you to be grouchy.
10. They think their business is not very important to you.

Unreasonable expectations include:

1. They think you should accept sexual or racial harassment.
2. They think you should accept unruly behaviour from them or their children.
3. They think you will deal with them under the table.
4. They think you can spend a lot of unproductive time with them.
5. They think they are always right.
6. They think you should accept physical threats or bullying.
7. They think you have been trained to take advantage of them.
8. They think you have to cater to their every whim.
9. They think they are more important than all of your other customers.

10. They think you, personally, are responsible for all of their problems.

No two customers, it seems, have identical expectations of you or your store. Some customers like you immediately and become loyal, while others take an instant dislike to you, and become cool and distant. Some think you're an idiot; some think you're a hero. Some come in expecting the best; others expect the worst.

As I've suggested, there are many factors that contribute to these expectations. They fall into five basic categories: needs, personal situations, circumstances, personalities, and predispositions.

CUSTOMERS' NEEDS

Every customer who comes into your store comes in with a need. For most, it is a positive need that ultimately leads to a purchase. Our Customers from Hell often have a different set of needs. They need to return merchandise. They need to let you know that they may have paid too much for something. They need reassurance. They need to see a demonstration of something before they buy it. They need to make somebody else happy with their purchase. They need to purchase something that is out of stock. They need a bargain.

A "negative need," such as having to return something or being in a hurry when there's a long line-up, is an obvious breeding ground for conflict. But even a "positive need," such as having to purchase a gift for a niece's wedding, can result in conflict if that need goes unfulfilled. These needs, both positive and negative, are established long before your customer sets foot in your store. They are very real, totally beyond your control, and play a significant role in generating conflict.

You may not want to hear this, but a significant amount of our suffering with Customers from Hell is self-induced. Very often we, not the customer, unwittingly plant the seeds of conflict. As will be discussed in greater detail later on, one of the common mistakes made by well-meaning salespeople is to misinterpret a customer's need, which can create frustration and lead to conflict.

One spring, for example, I set out to purchase a new set of golf clubs. Now, I should point out that the only thing keeping me from a career as a professional golfer is that I stink at the game. I love it with a passion, but it has never loved me back. I figured, though, that maybe I could begin improving my game by improving the equipment I was using. Problem was, I really had no idea how to select a set of clubs. I needed expert advice.

My first stop was a reputable golf-equipment dealer that carried a large selection of clubs. I had no sooner entered the store than a smiling young man approached me and offered to help. He led me through the aisles of bags, carts, and other unidentifiable (to me) stuff, then gestured to a wall displaying no fewer than fifty sets of clubs.

"Here they are," he announced proudly, then stepped back to let me look around.

Overwhelmed, I confided to him that I really had no idea what I was looking for and would appreciate some suggestions.

"Sure," he said obligingly. "Approximately how much did you want to spend?"

I explained to him that money wasn't really an issue, but that I wanted a good set of clubs that would serve me well. This seemed to confuse him a little.

"Well, they're all good clubs," he said finally. "Some of them are just engineered a little differently."

That's a big help, I thought to myself, then aloud I asked, "Well, what, for instance, is the difference between this set for $1,400 and that set for $250?"

"Oh, well, the $1,400 set is made out of different material and weighted a little differently, that's all," he replied without hesitation.

"Oh, okay," I said uncertainly. I migrated to the more expensive clubs, working on the assumption that they would be better quality. I was handling an $1,100 set when the salesperson chirped, "We do have a set on sale right now — regularly $450, now on for $350. It's a great bargain."

"Really," I said, without a lot of enthusiasm, then followed him to the clubs. "Are they as good as those $1,100 ones?" I walked back to the more expensive sets.

He ignored my question and instead told me of another set of clubs, also on sale for $350. Again I looked at them, and again I walked back to the other clubs. Twice more during our encounter he dragged me away from the more expensive sets to offer me the low-end products. I ended up walking out in quiet frustration.

The young salesperson lost a sale and completely frustrated me because he failed to listen to and acknowledge my needs. I wanted a good-quality set of clubs that suited my purposes; he wanted to sell me something cheap. He assumed I was looking for a bargain. He assumed my needs were the same as his, or perhaps the same as his last customer's. That misinterpretation and my ensuing frustration could easily have led to a confrontation. Fortunately, because I'm just such an all-around wonderful person, all that happened was that he lost a sale.

CUSTOMERS' PERSONAL SITUATIONS

A former colleague of mine, whom I had worked with for several years, was once faced with a gut-wrenching conflict of loyalties. A disaster had occurred with a major project she was working on for one of our clients. To correct it, she and her entire group were going to have to work well into the night. To make matters worse, that evening she was supposed to embark on her much-delayed honeymoon. Her plane tickets were non-refundable, and even a reimbursement by the company could not remedy the fact that her husband would be unable to recover his vacation time.

While she was brooding on her predicament, she was approached by her executive V.P. He began to discuss minor corrections to some work she had done on an earlier project. She exploded, and launched into a twenty-minute tirade that was heard throughout the office. Until that time, I had never heard her raise her voice, lose her cool, or say an unkind word to anyone. But we all have a threshold — even those of us who are wonderful.

One of the great truths of life is that at any given time, we are all under some degree of stress. Sometimes that stress is positive and productive; other times it is negative and destructive. The nature and degree of this stress plays a very large part in our daily behaviour.

Fortunately, the personal situations of our customers don't often significantly affect our dealings with them. Someone may be a little grouchier or a little happier or a little quieter than normal, but it's usually not enough to distress us. When one of our customers is experiencing a situation that is extraordinarily negative, however, and enters our store with the corresponding stress, it may not take much of anything to trigger erratic behaviour.

A negative situation can include personal trouble with a husband or a wife, a divorce, the loss of somebody close, the loss of a job, the stress of a job, and so on. Many of us have experienced financial stress: a bounced cheque, a rejected credit card, a broken-down car with no money to fix it.

In fact, there are as many different kinds of stress producers as there are people. Some people can experience intense stress simply by discovering lint on their clothing. Others can go through disastrous situations seemingly unfazed.

It has been said that customers have become more demanding over the past few years, but I'm not sure that "demanding" is the right word. Apprehensive, maybe. Certainly more cautious. But why shouldn't they be? The world is becoming an increasingly stressful place in which to live, and that stress affects everything we do.

As salespeople, we have no control over our customers' personal situations. Nor do we, in any real sense, have any way of understanding their personal situations before we come in contact with them. We need to remember, though, that a customer's personal situation can, and often does, play a significant role in conflict. Even the most pleasant people, when caught in a desperate position, can react and interact badly.

THE CIRCUMSTANCES

The very circumstances of your contact with a customer can be the cause of conflict. Perhaps a hurried customer is forced to wait in a long line-up. Maybe she simply can't afford to purchase the item she desperately needs. Maybe you need a manager's authorization to process a return, and the manager is at lunch. Maybe the customer's credit card is maxed out.

Sometimes the unpleasant circumstances in which we find ourselves are caused by a salesperson (maybe even you) not having done her job properly in the first place. Sometimes the circumstances are a result of ill-conceived company planning and policies. No-return or exchange-only policies, as will be discussed towards the end of the book, just beg for conflict. Hotel restaurants are notorious for being understaffed, resulting in excruciatingly slow service, which in turn results in conflict. Some jewellery stores make a practice of hiding price tags (to force customers to approach salespeople), which inevitably irritates people.

But even in the best of retail stores, awkward circumstances can arise: a computerized cash system goes down; an unexpected throng of customers shows up when you're understaffed. It seems to be a part of retail life.

Whatever the cause of the circumstances, it's the person on the front line who is faced with the dissatisfied customer.

What makes these circumstances especially difficult is that they are typically stressful for both the salesperson and the customer. Sometimes the temptation for you, as the salesperson, is to say, "Look, buddy, this isn't easy for me either!" (which isn't recommended). The customer usually has a legitimate right to be dissatisfied. You may have a right to be dissatisfied too, but that's not your customer's problem.

Whenever I hear a salesperson insisting on standing up for her rights when she's with a customer, I think of a wonderful old piece of doggerel my parents taught me. It's also quoted in Dale Carnegie's masterpiece, *How to Win Friends and Influence People,* so it must be good.

> *Here lies the body of Johnny Grey,*
> *Who insisted on taking his right of way.*
> *He was right, dead right, as he sped along,*
> *But he was just as dead as if he were wrong.*

Recognizing and Defusing
Potentially Negative Circumstances

Some circumstances are natural breeding grounds for conflict. Sometimes the conflict is inevitable, but often we have the opportunity to minimize it with our very first words and actions. Here are some of the negative circumstances in which we commonly find ourselves, as well as some strategies for minimizing the conflict.

Declined Credit Card

You've rung up the purchase. The customer is standing in front of you, and there are two people behind him in line.

You swipe his credit card through the machine, and the card is declined. What do you do?

If you are like most retail people, you say one of the following:

- "I'm sorry, sir, but your credit card has been declined."
- "Ummm, there appears to be a problem with your credit card."
- "I'm sorry, sir, but yergunnahafta use a different method of payment."
- "There seems to be some sort of problem . . . Let me just try it again."

None of these strategies is as productive as it could be, and each has the effect of embarrassing your customer. These strategies make difficult circumstances worse.

The customer may now feel compelled to explain what's happened or, equally likely, will express outrage that his card was declined. He might direct his emotion at you. Even though he might have been expecting the card to be turned down, he will try to minimize his embarrassment by attempting to convince you (and the other customers around you) that there has been a terrible mistake.

You will never be able to completely eliminate your customer's embarrassment, but you can minimize it, and any ensuing conflict, by trying one of the following approaches instead:

▶ Hand the card back and say quietly, "Do you have another card you would prefer to use?"

▶ Hand the card back and say quietly, "We've been having a little trouble with our machine lately. Do you have another card you would prefer to use?"

▶ Hand the card back and say quietly, "Oh, these stupid machines! Do you have another card you would prefer to use?"

In each of these examples, the salesperson is maintaining control by asking a question of the customer. Specifically, the question is designed to direct the customer to a positive action. Examples 2 and 3 are intended to give your customer an "out" to help him preserve his dignity. Any one of these approaches will help minimize a stressful situation.

No-Refund Policy

A store has a no-refund policy, but a customer is returning a product and wants a refund. The typical salesperson's responses are:

- "I'm sorry, exchange or credit note only."
- "We don't give refunds. Yergunnahafta exchange it."
- "I'm sorry, but it says right on your receipt that there are no refunds."
- "I'm afraid we have a bit of a problem — we have a no-refund policy."

These are classic examples of "negative language" — phrases that use negative terminology. You're always better off trying to present things with a positive spin. For example:

▶ "Our store has a terrific exchange policy. What have you seen that has caught your eye?"

▶ "Unfortunately, the store doesn't give cash refunds — but we do have a great exchange or credit-note policy. What have you seen that has caught your eye?"

▶ "I'd love to refund this, but this store has a great exchange or credit-note policy instead. What have you seen that has caught your eye?"

As I did with the example of the declined credit card, I'm recommending that the salesperson gently outline the situation, then take control by asking a question of the customer. This helps direct the customer towards making a proactive decision.

When you fail to take control — when, for example, you say something like "I'm sorry, exchange or credit note only," without following it with a question — the unintended implication is, "So what are you going to do about it, bub?" This is at best an unproductive response and at worst a confrontational one.

Unusual Delays or Long Line-Ups

Your customer is in a hurry and has had to wait in line for fifteen minutes before you get to him. You're a waitress in a busy restaurant, the kitchen is running a little slow, and people are starting to get a tad grouchy.

> When people are in a hurry, the last thing you should worry about is how fast you are going.

Typically, the salesperson gets focused on increasing her speed and efficiency. She puts her head down and concentrates on the cash register in hopes that the customers will realize she is, in fact, working as fast as she can. Her face screws up and hardens, and her voice becomes clipped and mechanical. Her body language screams out, "I'm working as fast as I can, but don't you dare mess with me. I could just lose it!"

This may sound a little odd, but one of the great secrets of customer service is that when people are in a hurry, the last thing you should worry about is how fast you are going. I learned this lesson from Margaret, a friend and former employee in one of my toy stores. Margaret is, without question, one of the most highly skilled "people persons" I have ever had the pleasure of meeting. She is a tremendous salesperson, and was an invaluable asset to my company.

Margaret's only "weakness," as near as I could figure, was that she had very little patience for things even remotely mechanical. Pocket calculators were a minor challenge; the multi-line phone system was a constant source of stress for her; and she almost quit when I brought in a computerized cash-register system.

Margaret was working alone in the store one late November day. Two other employees were having lunch, and I had disappeared to meet with a supplier in the mall restaurant. Shortly after I arrived at the restaurant, the manager came over and told me that I was needed at the store. "Apparently the cash register isn't working," he said.

As I quickly walked back to the store, I envisioned a frantic Margaret facing down a Christmas rush of impatient and unpleasant customers. When I added to that the stress of a misbehaving computerized cash register, I fully expected to find her curled up in a fetal position in the middle of the store.

As I got closer, I could see through the entrance more than a dozen customers lined up at the cash register. I had a vivid image of what Margaret's letter of resignation was going to look like. But to my great surprise (and delight), I saw as I entered the store that the customers were anything but grouchy. Quite the opposite, in fact. I felt as though I had walked into a party.

Margaret, instead of trying to hide from the problem, had decided to manage it by entertaining the customers. She had them joking with each other and laughing out loud. By the time I arrived, she was in the process of walking up and down the line, soliciting suggestions on words to describe the computer. Everyone was having a great time.

When Margaret spotted me marching towards her, she announced in a voice loud enough for everyone to hear: "Shaun, we have decided that the following best describes your stupid computer: it is unreliable, ignorant, rude, offensive, garbage . . . and stupid!"

While everyone was laughing, Margaret turned to me and said under her breath, with deadly seriousness, "Fix the damn thing!" She then turned back to the troops and continued her entertaining while I got the computer up and running again. (It turned out she had simply forgotten to hit the Enter key, but I never had the heart to tell her!)

Margaret made the best of a bad situation. So much so, in fact, that customers were still joking about it years later.

What would most of us have done? We would have just stood there, apologizing to the customers, letting the stress build up. We'd have panicked. Some of us would have got angry. The lesson I learned that day is that customers are far more interested in how well they are treated than in how quickly they are processed.

You Don't Have an Advertised Item in Stock
The feature item in your store's sales flyer didn't show up on time. The store didn't receive the full shipment. The manager didn't order enough. Whatever the case, you now have a steady stream of grouchy customers demanding to know how your store has the audacity not to have the advertised product in stock.

Here are some of the things I've heard from the mouths of salespeople:

- "Sir, I just work here."
- "I don't know when they'll be showing up. Yergunnahafta keep checking."
- "Sorry." [*Shrugs*.]
- "The only thing I can do is give you a rain check."

Each of these responses suggests to the customer that it's his problem, not yours, and each focuses on the negative aspects of the situation.

If you find yourself in this situation, try something proactive, such as "I wish I could tell you I had one for you, but unfortunately the item hasn't shown up yet. Would you like me to give you a rain check, would you like to drop by tomorrow to see if it has shown up, or would you like me to give you a call when it comes in?"

By asking such questions, you have re-established control, changing the customer's focus from the problem to a pro-active decision.

CUSTOMERS' PERSONALITIES

Every interaction with a customer involves dealing with that customer's unique personality (not to mention yours). As discussed, this is often the focus for conflict-management techniques. And it is, in truth, a significant factor in generating and resolving conflict.

Analyzing an individual's behaviour is really the closest we can come to understanding his or her personality. As I've pointed out, however, an individual's behaviour during a conflict is not necessarily an accurate measure of his or her personality. Anyone can, at one time or another, exhibit unpleasant behaviour. In a three- or four-minute conflict situation, we might assess someone as a hostile/aggressive, Type-A personality, when she is actually a typically passive person in absolutely desperate need.

There are unquestionably highly effective and proven techniques for dealing with specific personality types. These are quite appropriate for resolving ongoing conflict in the workplace, where over time you have the opportunity to gain a better understanding of a person. However, in a conflict situation with a customer, somebody with whom you may have had little or no previous contact, you do not have the time or enough information to make a judgement about that individual's personality. Even if you did have the skill and intuition to accurately pinpoint someone's personality type in two or three minutes, that's only part of the battle. You still have to develop a workable strategy for dealing with that personality type, and plan the appropriate responses. That requires time that you simply don't have, and planning that, in a stressful environment, is very challenging indeed.

Perhaps the greatest mistake made in gauging the personality of others is to assume that everyone else is, or should be, more or less like you. The last time I counted, there were several billion people on this planet, each with a unique personality. Your perception of someone's personality is not based on some objective, universal standard, because there isn't one. Your perceptions come directly from the viewpoint of your own personality. You may, for instance, perceive someone as oversensitive while they perceive you as insensitive. Who's right? Who's wrong? Neither one of you.

Personality, nonetheless, is a significant factor in any conflict, and so it is something that we, as salespeople, must be aware of. There will be times when, no matter what we do, a conflict we are handling keeps escalating. Personality is often the random element that can thwart your best efforts.

CUSTOMERS' PREDISPOSITIONS

The final piece of baggage a customer carries into our store is a set of predispositions, or pre-existing beliefs. In other words, before the customer has even spoken with you, he may already have a set of ideas about either the store or you personally. Unfortunately, these ideas may not be working in your favour. Customers may believe they're going to get a hassle, for example. They may believe that someone who works in retail will be too stupid to resolve a problem. They may think you are going to try to cheat them. They may believe that you are not honest. They may believe that you are agreeing with their selections only because you are paid to agree with their selections.

Have you ever anticipated having a problem with someone and pre-planned what you were going to say — your "script" — before you met with him or her? Sure you have. That's a result of predisposition. Predispositions can be caused by many different things, and like it or not we all have them. The most common types of predisposition are those we've developed through experiences. We draw conclusions from our personal experiences, and then project those conclusions onto future events.

Let's say, for instance, that you're in a mall and you enter three women's clothing stores in succession. In the first two stores, salespeople "pounce" on you (or so you perceive), badgering and hounding you, leaving you with the sensation of what we call pressure. As you prepare to enter the third store, how are you likely feeling? You may never have been in that store before, perhaps you've not even heard of it, but what is your emotional state as you cross the threshold? Apprehensive? A little fearful? What are you expecting from that salesperson who is walking towards you? Is it any wonder that customers will occasionally blurt out a frantic "I'm just looking!" before you've even said hello?

It doesn't have to take three or four repeated experiences for someone to develop a predisposition. Ever heard the phrase "First impressions are lasting impressions"? We begin to establish our understanding of people, places, and things the first time we see them. For some people, a single experience is all it takes to form a virtually unshakeable opinion.

We all have predispositions. Some are created by prior experiences. Others have been taught by teachers and parents. The extreme of predisposition is, of course, prejudice. Racism, sexism, and ageism all affect our relationships with our customers. Think of the people around you — your friends, your family. What are their predispositions? Some people, for example, are predisposed to believe that a woman working in an electronics store will not have as much product knowledge or technical knowledge as a man working in the same store. Some women buying a new car are predisposed to believe that a male salesperson will not take them seriously or will treat them as if they are stupid. Some people are predisposed to believe that young people don't make good managers; some believe that older people don't make good managers.

Perhaps your customer has had an unpleasant experience in your store before, or knows somebody else who has. Perhaps he has a distrust of men or women in your occupation. Perhaps he believes that all retail salespeople care about is making a fast buck. Whatever predispositions your customers have, they are very real and can have a very real impact on the way they behave.

When you think about it, what I've painted here is a bleak,

distressing picture. The customer hasn't even walked in the door yet, and here he is with a set of expectations that we don't understand and can't influence — is it any wonder that we find conflict so difficult and so stressful? Needs, a situation, the specific circumstance, a personality, and a predisposition — these five elements determine whether the customer enters your store with a set of expectations that are positive or negative. These expectations, when combined with your response, determine whether there will be conflict and whether that conflict will become a confrontation.

The essence of resolving conflict is to first separate the expectations that lead to the conflict from the behaviour that fuels it, and then to work to understand those expectations. Our natural tendency is to react to the customer's behaviour, which simply doesn't work. Conflict resolution means taking positive action, not waiting for the customer to leave the store before you ask, "What's his problem?"

The vast majority of the customers we see every day, the satisfied customers, generally have a positive set of expectations. They expect certain things of us and our stores, we live up to those expectations, and a sale is made. But even when your customer has positive expectations, conflict can arise if those expectations are not met. Here's the formula in a nutshell:

A negative set of needs, situation, circumstance,
personality, and predisposition creates a negative expectation.
A negative expectation, when combined with a negative
response on your part, will create conflict.

Dealing with the Customer from Hell

A negative set of expectations and a positive response could cause a conflict to go either way, depending on the strength of the response. The same holds true for a positive set of expectations and a negative response.

Conflict begins with expectations. Your response determines whether the seeds of conflict take root, and the quality of your response depends entirely on your ability to understand those expectations.

Two

A Little Introspection:
Preventative Medicine

Before we start pointing our fingers
at our customers, we want to make darned
sure that the fingers shouldn't be pointed at us.

O ne of the recurring themes of this book will be that many of the difficult situations we encounter need never happen. Most difficult situations are born of customers who are frustrated by unfulfilled expectations caused by misguided store policies, a shortage of skill or motivation on the part of salespeople, or simply a lack of customer focus in the store. It only makes sense that trying to avoid self-inflicted wounds should be your first goal. But before concerning yourself with how to handle Customers from

Hell, let's make sure you're not creating them.

There are many things within the control of store managers and employees that can ensure greater customer satisfaction and help reduce conflict. Some are subtle, small suggestions and some are large, sweeping policy issues. The more of these you can deal with up front, the fewer challenges you will have to deal with in the long run. To give you an idea of what I mean, I have outlined what I consider to be the ten most important things you and your store can do to maximize customer satisfaction. Work on the ones you can control, and encourage other people to work on the ones over which you have no control.

1. *Become a better salesperson.*
Read the next chapter, "A Salesperson's Mission," a couple of times and encourage your fellow employees to do the same. If you are an employer, bring in a strong sales trainer or a sales training program. Make sure it is something that will have a measurable effect on the sales floor. Try to avoid videotapes, posters on the wall, buttons, and fancy slogans. Bring in a program that increases people's skills. The pleasant side-effect of training, of course, is that it can significantly increase your sales.

2. *Have a hassle-free, money-back return policy.*
A good friend of mine has an immensely successful retail store that does well in excess of a million dollars in sales every year. He credits a good portion of that success to having changed his return policy from a thirty-day exchange or credit to a

completely hassle-free, money-back policy. An awful lot of unpleasant customer encounters are created by restrictive return policies.

Yes, I understand the rationale behind these restrictive return policies, but for the most part that rationale represents acute short-term thinking. An average customer shops in your store eight times a year and remains within your target market for ten years. That's eighty purchases. If each purchase averages fifty dollars, you've made $4,000 in sales from that one customer. To me, it doesn't make sense to risk losing $4,000 of business for a fifty-dollar item, not to mention the severe repercussions to be had when that upset customer expresses her discontent to her circle of friends.

3. *Lose the negative signage.*

I remember pulling into a roadside restaurant after driving a fairly long stretch of highway. As I pulled in, there was a big sign in the parking lot that said No Dogs. Another sign ten feet away warned Trespassers Will Be Prosecuted. Ten feet from that was a sign that said No Buses.

As I got to the front door, there were three more signs. One said No Shirt, No Shoes, No Service, another one said Washrooms for Restaurant Patrons Only, and the last one said No Take-Out During Busy Times. Inside, at the cash, another sign said No Personal Cheques. Several months later, when I passed by again, there was a new sign out front. It read Out of Business.

Sometimes we get frustrated that our customers aren't reading our "rules," so we make our signs bigger and blunter, underline the noes, and make bold our key points. The few customers who actually do read your signs will find them angrily written and highly offensive.

The truth is, most customers don't bother reading — they're busy looking at your inventory. If there are signs you feel you must have, look carefully at the way they are worded. For example, a sign that says No Refunds, Exchange Only, Receipt Required would be far better reading something like this: "We want our customers to be happy. If you have any problems whatsoever, bring in your product and your receipt, and we will be delighted to exchange it."

Remember: negative signage creates a negative atmosphere, and a negative atmosphere nurtures conflict.

4.   *Remove "Yergunnahafta" from your vocabulary.*
Be conscious of the way you say things to people. Customers don't gunnahafta do anything. There is always a better way to say things. (I will get into this in more detail in the next chapter.)

5.   *Don't start closing the doors to your store early.*
Walk through a shopping centre at fifteen minutes before closing and see how many retailers have their doors half closed. The signal to the customers is clear: go away; you are a nuisance; we don't care. For the customer who is desperate to make a last-minute purchase in your store, the "you're not wanted" message might be the last straw.

6.   *Don't advertise things you don't have.*
Many retailers believe that price is the biggest issue for today's

consumer. That is not the case. A national survey conducted in 1995 ranked price third among customer beefs. In first place was poor customer service and spot two went to a store not having what it advertised in a sales flyer. Be forewarned: the days of "bait and switch" are over, and "just in time" inventory systems are worthwhile only when they are, in fact, in time.

7. *Never, ever promise something you can't deliver.*
Never let a customer have higher expectations for your product than the product can actually deliver. It's great to make a sale, but lousy to lose a customer.

8. *Make sure your prices are well marked.*
Don't use convoluted and confusing pricing games, such as "Buy Two and Get the Third One for Half-Price!" If you're going to have a sale, have a sale, for crying out loud.

Some stores intentionally leave prices off their merchandise, in the belief that this will force customers to talk to a salesperson. It is just as likely to frustrate them, causing them to walk out the door.

9. *Avoid cutesy advertising.*
We've all seen the signs:

GOING OUT for BUSINESS SALE

or

It's Not a

BANKRUPTCY SALE,
but It's Just as Good as One.

Advertising like this may sound very clever to you, but your customers will find it very deceptive — and rightly so. You may think this kind of advertising is cute, but your customers don't. No one likes to feel as if he has been tricked. It may bring you business in the short term, but when you lose a customer's trust and respect, you lose business in the long term.

10. *Empower your employees.*
Give your employees the authority to make decisions on the sales floor. No customer enjoys being told, "You're gunnahafta talk to my manager." If you are entrusting an employee with the success of your store, whether that employee is full time or part time, why in heaven's name would you not give him or her the tools to do the best job possible?

If you don't believe that your employees have the capacity to make good decisions, then you've hired poorly. Yes, even your best employees will make mistakes when you empower them. And some of those mistakes will cost you money in the short term. In the long term, though, your customers, your employees, and you will all be happier. Nothing is more productive than a strong, trusting work environment.

· · · · · · · · ·

THREE

A Salesperson's Mission

· ·

The better the job we do as salespeople,
the fewer challenges we have with customers.

· ·

O kay, okay, I know — I'm supposed to be talking about Customers from Hell here, not salespeople. But I think it's important that we agree on what customers should be able to expect of you. A lot of the conflict encountered with customers would simply never happen if salespeople lived up to customers' expectations. Although this book is about managing difficult customers, I think we all know that conflict rarely has only one side to it.

So how can you be sure that it's not you who's causing the

problems? How can you keep from unwittingly becoming the Salesperson from Hell? What can you use as a benchmark to evaluate your performance in terms of your relationships with your customers? I believe that the job of a retail salesperson can be broken down into six different elements, six things that make the difference between really good salespeople and the plain, average salespeople we encounter every day. These elements contribute to what I think should be the mission of every salesperson: *to provide the most positive experience possible to every customer who comes into the store.*

I have encountered many fine retail salespeople over the years, and if there is one thing that is common to all of them it is this sense of mission. It is the customer-oriented attitude. They never forget that the ultimate goal is always customer satisfaction.

All too often we find ourselves getting caught up in the mundane, day-to-day support tasks of restocking shelves, dusting, tidying, vacuuming, facing shelves, inventory control, and cash balancing. We bring our personal problems to work. We begin to lose focus. We begin to take our customers for granted — or worse, we begin to think of them as nuisances.

In each of my toy stores, I had a plaque hanging on the wall that said:

This country has no resource greater than its children.
No one has greater wealth than one who has a child.
And there is no greater tragedy than a child who has been
    denied his or her future.
If we can help just one child grow to be a better person,

Then we have achieved our objective.
If we can make just one unhappy child happy,
Then we have made a profit.

I believed this adage when I wrote it, and I believe it now. Throughout all the challenges and stresses we face each day, we must never lose sight of our commitment to our customers. So what are the six key functions of a really good salesperson?

1. A salesperson sells.
2. A salesperson makes customers comfortable.
3. A salesperson is an ambassador for the company.
4. A salesperson is always positive.
5. A salesperson is always honest.
6. A salesperson cares.

Let's take a closer look at these key functions one at a time.

FUNCTION #1: A SALESPERSON SELLS

Is this profound, or what? The first function of a salesperson is to sell. In other words, we are not being paid just to stand behind a counter and wait for people to make their selection and hand over their money. In this day and age, this is unacceptable, not just to the owners of our businesses but to our customers as well.

You may consider selling to be a rather obvious part of a salesperson's job, but to many people — believe it or not — "selling" is somehow considered inappropriate behaviour in a retail store. Frightening, but true. To be fair, the people who tend to feel negatively about selling really don't have a good handle on what selling is all about. They think of selling as something . . . well, unwholesome. They think of selling as someone "doing something" to someone else.

Our role as salespeople who actually sell reflects a change from the way retail used to be. In the past, we've used terms like "clerk," "customer service representative," and "consultant," and some companies even had the audacity to call their salespeople "assistant buyers" (because the salespeople, of course, assist customers in making a good purchase). When I began conducting retail programs many years ago, only about half of the employees who attended considered themselves salespeople. Fortunately, this is now changing.

As a retail salesperson, you should assume that everyone who walks into your store needs or wants something. Everyone — even people who are "just browsing" — comes in with a need or a want. It may not be a specific need — it may not even be a current need — but something got them out of bed that morning and got them out shopping. They chose to turn into your store instead of the store next door or the store across the hall because they believe you have, or may have, the answer to that need or want.

"What about when customers are just browsing?" you may ask. Fair question. Think for a moment about your own routine. You've finished your shopping and have some time to kill. You begin wandering around the mall, peering in at the storefront displays. Some stores you don't enter, some you do. Since you don't have anything specific in mind, what was it that motivated you to turn into these particular stores?

If you had friends with you, chances are they would not have been drawn to exactly the same stores as you. What's motivating them?

We browse only in those stores that attract us. And they attract us primarily because of the inventory they carry — inventory that we either typically purchase or aspire to purchase. We may not have an immediate need, or a clearly defined need, but the need is very much there nevertheless, and salespeople should never lose sight of it.

One of the great limiting factors in retail today is that many salespeople work under assumptions that are neither proactive nor productive. For example, some salespeople believe that customers prefer to be left to their own devices, without a salesperson's "interference." Others assume that customers have absolutely no intention of buying. I'll never forget one two-hour coaching session I had with four middle-aged salespeople in a junior department store, trying to persuade them to say hello to their customers. They were adamantly convinced that their customers would find this a distasteful intrusion into their shopping experience. Needless to say, this store — in fact, the whole chain — has struggled.

What Is Selling?

We talk about "selling," but what is it really? What exactly differentiates a salesperson who sells from one who does not?

Selling can be broken down into four basic activities: greeting the customer, probing/discovering the customer's needs, presenting the product, and closing the sale. Different training programs, of course, use different terminology, and some programs include many more steps, but these four are the basics. The basics are what contribute the most to positive sales growth and positive customer experiences. And it is with the basics that retail salespeople are most likely to trip up.

Greeting the Customer
The first sales step, and therefore the first responsibility of a salesperson, is to greet customers — every single customer who comes into the store. Customers need to feel appreciated, and a simple hello from you can make all the difference in the world.

The concept of greeting a customer is obvious. It's almost so logical and self-evident that it doesn't warrant discussion. But as obvious as it may seem to you that greeting a customer is part of a salesperson's job, I challenge you to walk through a shopping centre without passing dozens and dozens of salespeople who are task-oriented — putting product on shelves, pricing things, walking around with clipboards — and thus totally ignoring the customers who pass them by.

All it takes to greet a customer is "Hi," "Good morning," "Good afternoon," or "Good evening." But this has to be initiated by the salesperson, not the customer. It's not hard to do — there's no magic involved. Greeting customers is perhaps the simplest activity salespeople perform, and yet our research indicates that fewer than 30 percent of employees in retail stores greet their customers well. Scary, huh?

Probing/Discovering
After saying hello to a customer, the next activity of a salesperson is to learn as much as he can about that customer —

to discover what it is that she needs, or why she is in the store. Through skilful questioning and attentive listening, the salesperson must determine not only the customer's intellectual needs, but her emotional needs as well.

Although this discovery process is one of the cornerstones of salesmanship, it is not as widely practised in retail as it should be. The vast majority of retail salespeople are content to let their customers browse or, conversely, to follow them around the store. Those who aren't ignoring their customers spend their time answering questions or spouting off reams of information instead of taking control (as the experts they are) and asking the questions that will determine their customers' needs.

Does the discovery process really make a difference? You bet. Take a look at how a typical sales interview might go without the salesperson probing to determine a customer's needs:

Customer: Do you sell flip charts?
Salesperson: No, I'm afraid we're all out.
Customer: Crumb. Any idea where I might get one?
Salesperson: Well, you can try Paula's Presentation Palace. I know they usually carry them.
Customer: They're all the way across town!
Salesperson: Yeah, I know. There may be someplace closer, but I'm not sure where.
Customer: Okay. Well, thanks anyway . . .

Sound familiar? Sure it does. This is typical of many sales situations. The customer asks questions and the salesperson does her best to answer them, but neither the customer nor the salesperson ends up with her needs satisfied.

Here's the same interview, this time with the salesperson discovering a little about her customer by asking a few probing questions:

Customer: Do you sell flip charts?

Salesperson: [*Probing*] No, I'm afraid we're all out. What did you need it for?

Customer: Well, I'm doing a seminar today, and I realized that I've got nothing to write on.

Salesperson: [*Probing*] Oh, wow, you are in a bind. And the nearest place I know of to get a flip chart is right across the city. Let's see . . . how do you typically use the flip chart?

Customer: I use it to write down the key points I make, so that those in the audience can then copy it down at their leisure. I just don't know what I'm going to do without one.

Salesperson: [*Probing*] Does it have to be a flip chart?

Customer: What were you thinking?

Salesperson: Well, we don't have flip charts in stock, but we do have some white-board easels. You know, the ones that use the dry-erase markers? They're a little more expensive than a flip chart, but they'll do the same job.

Customer: That would be perfect. Can I take a look at them?

The salesperson in the first example was polite, helpful, and well-meaning, but she didn't take the time to understand her customer or her customer's *needs*. As a result, she lost a sale and forced her customer to drive across town for a solution she had right in her own store. The salesperson in the second example asked three simple questions, made a sale, and saved her customer a lot of grief.

Customers usually have a pretty good idea of what their needs are when they come into your store, but they rarely have the wealth of product knowledge that you have. If you don't ask them appropriate questions — as a doctor does with a patient, for example — your customers can't benefit from your expertise.

A customer in one of my toy stores once marched into my office three days after Christmas and slammed a product down on my desk, furiously declaring it to be the absolute and totally wrong thing for her four-year-old child. She was livid, loud, and very unpleasant. She had spent more than $200 on a product she had picked out herself, and her child's Christmas was, in her opinion, ruined. It was difficult to disagree. The toy was designed for a child ten to thirteen years old.

By not adequately discovering the needs of this customer, the salespeople in the store at the time she selected this product had fallen down on the job — and the result was a spoiled Christmas for a little girl (and her mother). Did the customer have a right to be upset, even though she had picked out the product herself? Absolutely. Who was to blame? We were.

Presenting the Perfect Product
The third step of the sales process is for the salesperson to identify the perfect product based on what she has learned of the customer, and then present that product to the customer.

This requires a thorough knowledge of the products in the store, as well as their features and benefits. It is also the part of the process where the customer is depending on the salesperson to make a firm and appropriate recommendation.

Selling a customer the wrong product is a recipe for conflict. Nothing can dissolve a customer's trust in us faster than an exhibition of poor product knowledge or an inappropriate recommendation. I have suggested that perhaps the most common error salespeople make is to second-guess customers' needs. At the presentation stage of the sales process, we are in the most danger of paying the price of making inaccurate assumptions about people.

One of our clients is a large national cellular-phone service provider. I was coaching the salespeople in one of this client's stores when a man came in looking for a cellular phone. The customer was young, casually dressed in jeans and a T-shirt, and appeared to have little knowledge about the products. Even though the customer said that he required the phone for business and would likely be using it on a fairly frequent basis, the salesperson sold him a starter package that featured a low monthly base fee but had high air-time costs. The rationale for this, the salesperson explained to me, was that he didn't feel the young customer would be able to support the higher monthly fee of some of the premium packages. When I pointed out that the premium packages offered substantially lower air-time rates, which would be more appropriate for someone who would be using the phone a lot, the salesperson responded, "Yeah, but he's young, and the young ones tend to use the phones more on evenings and weekends, when the air time is free."

A couple of months later, I discovered that the customer had returned to the branch after receiving his first bill, extremely angry with the salesperson. His phone bill was almost three times what it would have been had he received the right package in the first place. The salesperson learned the hard way a lesson about second-guessing his customers.

Closing the Sale
The final step in the sales process, closing the sale, is unquestionably the least understood part. In the past, it has been described as "asking for the business" or "getting the customer to sign." It was viewed as the manipulative part of the sale, the point at which the salesperson "got the customer to do something." It's not surprising, then, that closing the sale has always been considered the hardest and least pleasant part of the sales process.

In truth, closing the sale is more about a salesperson saying or doing whatever he can to determine whether the customer has made a purchase decision. It's not as much about "asking for the business" as it is a matter of finding out if you're on the right track and bringing the sale to its logical conclusion.

Some of the best closing questions in the whole world are neither slick nor manipulative. Asking, for example, "Is this pretty much the sort of thing you had in mind?" gives a customer the opportunity to tell you how comfortable he is with your recommendation. More direct questions such as "Which of these colours do you prefer?" help customers focus on making a decision.

Unfortunately, very few retail people close sales well, if

they even do it at all. Most don't recognize this as part of the sales function, don't realize how important it is, or fear being perceived as "pushy." Of course, closing a sale is anything but pushy. Quite the contrary, it is critical to creating a comfortable relationship with a customer.

I was on my way to a seminar with a business associate one snowy, blustery day back in 1993. As we were walking from our hotel to the conference room, we passed by a streetfront menswear store. We had a little extra time, so we decided to go in and see what the store had. It was an elegantly appointed, upscale store with beautiful merchandise. My friend headed straight to a wall of sweaters while I was drawn to the selection of ties. On the rack was a tie that I had seen in Florida a couple of months earlier and had fallen in love with.

"Come here. Look at this," I hollered to my associate. "This is the tie. This is the one I've been telling you about. This is the most beautiful tie I've ever seen. I want this tie." Standing four feet away from me was the store manager, listening to our conversation.

Trouble was, I wasn't wearing the suit that the tie was to match. So I hemmed and hawed for a little bit and finally decided I'd forego the tie for now and drop in later when I was wearing the appropriate suit. The manager just stood there and said nothing. I, of course, never got the opportunity to go back, and to this day I have been kicking myself. The more I thought about it, the more I realized that I would have bought the tie if the salesman had closed the sale.

What were some of the subtle clues the manager got from me? "This is the tie." "This is the most beautiful tie I've ever seen." "I want this tie." Had the manager had the courage to simply say, "I agree. It's terrific. Would you like to look at some shirts to go with it?" I would be the proud owner of that tie. And after I had expressed my concern that it might not match my suit, he could easily have outlined his return policy and offered to give me a refund if it turned out not to be a good match. As it was, I walked away unsatisfied and the manager lost out on a $120 sale, thinking I was just another browser.

I think we've all, at some time or another, said, "Gee, I wish I'd bought that." The next time you say it, recognize it as a sign of a salesperson not having closed a sale.

And that, in a very tiny nutshell, is the sales process. Very simple, yet at the same time very challenging to execute well. Unfortunately, the process of selling is too often perceived as (and taught to be) a game in which the objective is to get as much money from the customer as possible. This idea is distasteful for most of us, and explains the negative images we associate with "salespeople."

Selling should be a process by which the salesperson does everything in her power to ensure that customers leave with their needs fulfilled. It is not a game, and there should be no losers. Effective selling always leads to a win-win conclusion, in which you and your customer each finish the sales interview a little better off than when you began. Your customer leaves the store without the burden of an unsatisfied need and you leave with fair financial reimbursement.

Skipping any one of the steps in the sales process will not lead to a win-win conclusion. In fact, missing a step can, and often does, set the stage for potential conflict.

FUNCTION #2: A SALESPERSON MAKES CUSTOMERS COMFORTABLE

The second function of the salesperson is to make customers comfortable. You want your customers to be relaxed, to feel at home and at ease, as if they are among friends.

I don't think many of us really ever go out of our way to make a customer feel uncomfortable. Yet most of us have made at least one of the classic mistakes that ends in that result. Sometimes we visit with our friends or co-workers when customers are in the store, making them feel like intruders. Sometimes we spout off rules and regulations that make our customers feel uncomfortable. Sometimes we badger and hound our customers. And worst of all, sometimes we just ignore them.

Making customers comfortable is easy to talk about, but not always easy to do. The challenge is that, to achieve a significant level of comfort for our customers, we often must sacrifice some of our own comfort.

"How many of you," I have asked in my seminars, "really and truly care about your customers' comfort?" Usually, around 90 percent of the hands in the room go up.

"Okay," I continue. "Now all of you who have ever started pulling the doors partway closed five or ten minutes early, put your hands down." About one-third of the hands go down.

"Now put your hands down if you have ever visited with friends or co-workers while there were customers in the store." Down go another bunch of hands.

"Anyone here start balancing the cash, only to have a customer show up? Anyone vacuum when the store is open?

Anyone chew gum while talking to customers?" By this time, few, if any, hands remain in the air.

Customer comfort means sometimes staying past closing time. It means asking your friends not to drop by or telephone when you're working. It means changing your routine to include some activities with which you may not now be comfortable.

Part of ensuring a customer's comfort is being very aware of your own verbal skills and body language. As we will cover in chapter 6, "Listening to Your Customer," the way you say things plays a huge role in how your customers behave. Even when your mouth's not talking, your body is, and it may not be sending the messages you intend. Do you cross your arms when you're talking to customers? Do you avoid eye contact? Do you slouch? If you do any of these things, you're saying, "I'm unreceptive, and I don't particularly care very much."

Do you always smile? (Note that I use the word "always." I'm not asking if you smile 60 percent of the time, or 70 or 80 percent of the time, but if you *always* smile when the customer is there.) We all know that smiling is important, and most of us think we smile, but a quick look through a shopping mall will show you how few people really do. Smiling is critical in retail; if you're not prepared to smile, then you'd best be prepared for grouchy customers. It doesn't count if you're just smiling inside, or even if you are smiling with your eyes. Smiling is a way of telling your customers that you care, and that you want them to be comfortable in your store.

FUNCTION #3: A SALESPERSON IS AN AMBASSADOR FOR THE COMPANY

The third function of a salesperson is to represent the company. Sometimes we forget that even when we're not wearing the company uniform or we're not working on the sales floor, we are still ambassadors for our store. We often, all too publicly, say negative things about our stores, our managers, and our environment without fully understanding the impact this has on our customers and our sales.

In fact, the indirect influence we have on the success of our stores is far greater than we realize. We all have friends and family who are loyal to us, and to whom we are loyal. They patronize our store, and encourage others to do so, because we work there. We do the same for them.

For twenty-four years, my brother worked as the information systems manager in the head office of one of Canada's most successful grocery chains. In those twenty-four years, as near as anyone can tell, he ate and drank and slept this company. He wore all of the company's promotional clothing. Many of the birthday and Christmas presents he and his wife gave people had the company's name stamped on them. And we all knew that if he came by for a visit and saw a bag from a competitive store lying around, we'd be in deep trouble indeed. He was the quintessential company man.

Think about this for a moment. How much revenue do you suppose my brother indirectly contributed to his company? It would be impossible to say for sure — I don't know if his sphere of influence is thirty people or 300 people — but I do know for a fact that over the years, my family alone purchased more than $20,000 worth of groceries from that company purely out of loyalty to my brother.

An experience I had a while back, while looking at cellular phones, stands in sharp contrast to the loyalty displayed by my brother. The company representative was exceptionally knowledgeable about cellphones and the programs and packages his company was offering. But when I told him the nature of my business and the way we expected to use the phones, he smiled and said, "Sir, we do have a package for you, but quite frankly, our competitor's package is far more attractive. I suggest you take a look at that one before you make your decision." I almost choked. Well intended though he might have been, he was doing more damage to his company than he knew. Not only was he biting the hand that fed him, but he was also positioning his company as inferior to his competition. How's that for setting himself up for potential future problems?

Always remember that every time you say something negative about your place of business, you are damaging your own credibility as well. Don't ever forget that people expect you to be an ambassador for your store.

FUNCTION #4: A SALESPERSON IS ALWAYS POSITIVE

The fourth function of a salesperson, which is closely related to the third, is to always be positive. How many times have you encountered a salesperson who speaks negatively about himself, a product, his company, or even worse, his customers? Remember the effect that salesperson's attitude had on your desire to shop in his store? It's not always easy to be positive, I realize, but if there is one universal truth it's that nobody likes a whiner. It doesn't matter at all how you perceive yourself. If customers perceive you as negative, then you will have conflict.

Often, the way customers perceive you has far less to do with what you say than with the way you say it. You really have to be aware of how you choose to phrase things. Imagine that you've just sat down for a drink at the local bar. The bartender comes up and says, "Whaddle it be?" You ask for a pint of your favourite ale, to which he replies, "We don't stock it. Yergunnahafta drink something else."

Now, technically, the bartender did nothing wrong. He, after all, didn't carry your brand. But did he make you feel comfortable? No. Is it possible you felt like you were being a bit of a pain in the rear? Yes. And while this situation alone might not have resulted in conflict, the sense of discomfort might easily have contributed to conflict later on. All because the bartender used negative language.

How could he have better said it? Well, how about something like this: "Good choice. Unfortunately, we're all out at the moment. What other brand can I interest you in?" By choosing his words carefully, he could have made you feel comfortable and welcome, and probably won himself a repeat customer.

There are a few words and phrases, negative language, that we hear a lot. The biggest offender is "yergunnahafta." Yergunnahafta is everywhere, and we've all heard it. See if you don't recognize some of these:

A Salesperson's Mission

In a restaurant:	"Yergunnahafta wait twenty minutes for a table."
For returning merchandise:	"Yergunnahafta show me the receipt."
For a special order:	"Yergunnahafta leave a deposit."
At an airline ticket counter:	"Yergunnahafta tuck the strap of your suitcase in."
In a busy store:	"Yergunnahafta wait until I'm finished with this customer."
For writing a cheque:	"Yergunnahafta show me two pieces of I.D."

Make a note to yourself. Customers don't *gunnahafta* do anything! Here's how the same things might be better expressed:

In a restaurant:	"We'll have a table ready for you in about twenty minutes."
For returning merchandise:	"Do you have your receipt?"
For a special order:	"We're all set, sir, and the deposit will be twenty dollars."
At an airline ticket counter:	"Could I get you to tuck in the strap of your suitcase?"
In a busy store:	"I'll be with you just as soon as I'm finished with this customer."
For writing a cheque:	"Do you have a driver's licence and perhaps a major credit card I can look at?"

There are many other forms of negative language, but I'm sure you get the idea. Don't believe, however, that negative language is used only by negative people. Listen to yourself. It's something we're all guilty of from time to time.

In addition to using negative language, we are also often guilty of unintentionally presenting positive things in a negative light. I'll never forget the time I was searching for a fax machine. I was looking at plain-paper machines, and when I asked how much they were, the salesperson replied, "They're pretty expensive. About $700."

Why did she say, "They're pretty expensive"? Why didn't she just say, "They're about $700"? Did she think I was cheap? Was she worried that I would complain about the price? I don't know. All I know is that the message I, the customer, received was this: "I don't think this is good value." And I'm not sure I want to shop in a store that doesn't provide good value.

A good salesperson thinks before speaking. You should always ask yourself two questions — What is the impact this will have on my customer? Is there a better, more positive way to say it? — before you open your mouth.

Remember: it's not what you say, but how you say it.

FUNCTION #5: A SALESPERSON IS ALWAYS HONEST

The fifth responsibility of a salesperson is to be honest, to have integrity. Trustworthiness is the hallmark of excellent salespeople and their companies.

In today's retail environment, honesty with customers is

part of our culture. But many fine salespeople are now suffering the after-effects of a time when making the sale seemed to come before all else. Salespeople in retail fashion, automotive, electronics, footwear, and furniture, to name only a few, often find customers questioning their sincerity and credibility.

You see, the philosophy not all that long ago was that you should never admit to any of your products' shortcomings, never question a customer's choice, and never do or say anything that might stand in the way of a sale. This "anything for a buck" mentality might have been considered good policy for short-term business, but it has haunted salespeople ever since.

As a rule of thumb, honesty means never promising what you can't deliver, never promising that a product will deliver what it cannot, and never promising that you will stand behind a product if you won't. Honesty, however, does not mean being insensitive. It is usually a good idea to temper your honesty with a little tact. If, for example, you work in a clothing store and someone comes out of the change room wearing something that looks terrible on her, don't say, "Well, that looks like a bag of dirt on you!" Try saying something more gentle, such as, "You know, we've got some other styles that I think may be more appropriate." The rule is to be honest, not brutal.

FUNCTION #6: A SALESPERSON CARES

I've left the most important function of the salesperson to the end, because without this one thing no store could ever survive: a salesperson has to care. Genuinely care about the customers. Genuinely care that customers are leaving with something they need. Genuinely care that customers have a problem that needs to be solved. Genuinely care that customers are always comfortable in the store.

Of all the employees I ever hired, perhaps the most impressive salesperson I had the pleasure of working with was a young lady named Beth. Now, Beth would die a thousand deaths if she knew I was referring to her in this book as a salesperson. She hated the label. To her the word "salesperson" dredged up images of the parasitic vacuum-cleaner salesman with a foot firmly wedged in the door or the used-car salesman who hasn't made a sale in two months. But while Beth didn't have sophisticated selling skills, she was in fact a salesperson, and an awesome one.

What she lacked in the technical aspects of selling she made up for with an overwhelming sense of caring for her customers. Beth cared deeply about making sure that her customers left with exactly what they needed. She was always concerned that perhaps she'd missed something or forgotten something. She never knew it, but the rest of us did — Beth was the soul of that store. When she left to go to school, the store's sales dropped, and I don't think it was a coincidence. The last I heard from her, she was teaching somewhere in Costa Rica. I often wonder if the parents of the children she's teaching appreciate what they've got.

We would all do well to take a page from Beth's book. Remember that eight out of ten customers who defect from your store, never to come back, leave because they thought you didn't care. They felt unappreciated. It's easy to say that you should care about your customer, but not so easy to do. It's difficult to care about everybody when there are tens of thousands of customers coming through the store every year. The only way to do it is to take your customers one at a time, deal with them one at a time, and care about them one at a time.

It is important that we talk in this book about the salesperson's job — *your* job — because any time you are in conflict, you are half of the equation. Before we start pointing our fingers at our customers, we want to make darned sure that the fingers shouldn't be pointed at us. In other words, before you start accusing your customers of being Customers from Hell, you have to ask yourself if you did your job properly. Did you follow all of the steps of the sales process? Was your customer comfortable the whole way through? Were you an ambassador for your company? Were you always honest with your customer? Were you always positive? If someone wanted to pay by cheque, did you say, "We'd be delighted to take your cheque, Mrs. Smith. Do you have a driver's licence I could take a look at, and perhaps a major credit card?" Or did you say, "Yeah, we can take a cheque. But yergunnahafta gimme two pieces of I.D." The difference in language is subtle, but the difference in effect is dramatic. And finally, did you really care? This is an important self-evaluation process to go through, because often those Customers from Hell aren't Customers from Hell at all. Sometimes the fault is with us. Yes, even you.

A "difficult customer" is very much in the eyes of the beholder. For instance, you may perceive someone to whom you are having difficulty making a sale as a difficult customer. But the problem may actually exist with your own skill level. I remember being stranded on the side of the road once with a flat tire. I had the car jacked up and was hopelessly struggling to remove the rusted lug nuts from the rim. I had spent twenty minutes on the stupid thing when a mechanic finally happened by. With three squirts of rust remover and a deft, sharp twist of the tire iron, the tire was off. Turned out that the tire wasn't difficult at all . . . at least, not for a person who knew what to do.

"I had a customer yesterday," a manager of a shoe store once told me in earnest, "who insisted on trying on every shoe in the store. I'll bet you I laced up twenty pairs of shoes on her feet. She was in the store for an hour and a half and simply could not make up her mind. Meanwhile, there were half a dozen other customers who went neglected. I probably get customers like that once a week, and they drive me nuts."

To the manager (Shirley), this woman was a Customer from Hell. But to me, the manager was a salesperson who, although quite motivated, wasn't doing her job as well as she should. I took the opportunity to ask her a few questions.

"What kind of clothes was she planning to wear with the shoes?"

"I don't know," Shirley replied.

I then asked, "What kind of heels did she say she preferred?"

"I don't know," she said again.

"Was she buying the shoes for a special occasion?" I persisted.

"I don't know," said Shirley, beginning to get exasperated with me. "She didn't tell me any of these things."

"Did you ask her any of these things?"

She paused for a moment and looked at me. "No," she said finally.

Here was a situation in which the customer had taken

complete control of the sales interview and had done so because Shirley, the salesperson, had not taken control. The salesperson had made no attempt to determine what the customer's needs were, and the customer, who lacked knowledge of the stock in the store, was attempting to qualify herself by trial and error.

I explained to Shirley that if she had perhaps taken the time to discover the woman's needs by asking her some probing questions, there was a chance that the sales interview might have been successfully conducted in considerably less time. Shirley's questions should have been about the clothes the customer would be wearing with the shoes, the occasion for which she was shopping, her colour preference, the style preferred, whether the shoes were being worn casually or for work, if she was looking for something for comfort or for aesthetics, and so on.

Shirley nodded at me, looking somewhat unconvinced. But she agreed that the next time she came across one of these customers, she would do as I suggested and see how it worked. Two weeks later, I was back in the store and she bounded up to me.

"It worked!" she said excitedly. "What you said worked. I had two of my most difficult customers just this week. I did exactly what you said, and I sold shoes to each of them in less than fifteen minutes. One of them even commented on how wonderful I was!"

To me, a customer for whom some extra effort is required is not a difficult customer. As our level of selling skill increases, the challenge presented by these customers decreases.

Am I expecting too much from someone who is "just a retail salesperson"? I don't think so. I strongly believe, and have told anybody who will listen, that retail today is one of the most difficult occupations out there. The skill sets required to survive and excel are numerous and diverse. The number of customers with whom we come into contact is staggering, far greater than in almost any other occupation. The training we receive is often minimal (or non-existent) and yet the expectations our customers have of us are high. Retail may very well be the most undervalued occupation on the planet.

Four

Controlling Your Emotions

The greater the emotional aspect of a conflict,
the more intense the level of confrontation.
The more intense the level of confrontation,
the more difficult the situation is to resolve.

I t's all very well and good to understand the theory of conflict, but it's another thing altogether to put it to use. We all know what really happens. Suddenly, the Customer from Hell is in our face. He is belligerent, or swearing, or lying, or trying to negotiate with us. He may be abusive, whining, impatient, or just plain loud. He is all of the things that drive us nuts.

Our initial response to this kind of behaviour is neither intellectual nor logical. It's instinctive. It comes from the gut.

I'm quite sure that I don't know anyone who could just sit back, listen to this kind of assault, and calmly ponder the theory of conflict. "Okay, let's see here. This person two inches from my face, screaming at me, has come in with a need, a situation, and a circumstance, coupled with a specific personality and predisposition. This has created within him a motivating set of expectations. Now how should I deal with this?"

It would be wonderful if we all had the capacity to be so dispassionate, but as *Star Trek*'s Mr. Spock puts it, "Humans are quite emotional, aren't they?" I think we all recognize the signs of emotion within us. Some of us feel the hair on the back of the neck starting to bristle. A sinking sensation in the stomach. A tingly feeling inside. The head may start to feel warmer. The breath may come a little faster. The heart rate goes up. Adrenaline begins coursing through the body as physiological defence mechanisms start to kick in. Fight or flight. This is the turning point for conflict. It is the point at which conflict can become confrontation.

Confrontation is a result of conflicting emotional states between two people. These emotional states must be addressed before the confrontation can be prevented or resolved. The greater the emotional aspect of a conflict, the more intense the level of confrontation. The more intense the level of confrontation, the more difficult the situation is to resolve. So regardless of the customer, regardless of the behaviour the customer is manifesting, regardless of the situation — the one critical first step you must take is to minimize the possibility and extent of confrontation.

There are really only three basic elements in managing any difficult situation:

1. Managing your personal emotional state.
2. Managing the other person's emotional state.
3. Solving the problem.

The purpose of the first two elements is to minimize the intensity and duration of any confrontation. The third element, solving the problem, is the intellectual part and is also, believe it or not, the easiest part of the process. This chapter focuses on strategies for the first element: managing your personal emotional state. It is essential that you master this if you hope to master conflict resolution.

Let's examine what happens in the first few seconds of a difficult situation. Think for a moment about the way you typically respond to crisis, stress, or conflict. Do you get angry and shout? Do you cry? Do you whine? Do you walk away? Do you cower to avoid the situation? Do you sulk? Do you snipe or take potshots at the other person? We all react instinctively, and chances are that you, like the rest of us, do not respond well. But can your reaction be controlled? Is it learned behaviour, or is it something we were born with?

I suggest to you that these are behavioural responses that we have learned and perfected throughout our lifetimes, and that we consequently have the ability to change. When we talk about managing emotions, what we are in reality talking about is managing the emotional state, the behaviour, the response to our emotions. It would be a mistake to believe that it is somehow a good thing for us to try to subvert or suppress our emotions, or pretend that they aren't there. That just doesn't work. Emotions such as fear, frustration, overwhelm, happiness, joy, and love are all very real. They are part of the human makeup. But the way that we respond to these emotions — with anger, rage, insecurity, sullenness, laughter, and so on — is all very controllable. You'll see that there are different ways to manage them.

How we react to our emotions is patterned behaviour. Our emotional states, and consequently our behaviour, are determined by specific triggers. The moment one of our "buttons" is pushed, the corresponding emotion is triggered and our predetermined behaviour pattern begins. Anthony Robbins, one of today's truly brilliant motivational speakers, perhaps describes the process the best. He uses the metaphor of a record playing in one's mind. (Remember records? Kind of like big CDs with holes in the middle.) When an emotional response is triggered, it is very much like a needle falling down on a record. The same old song starts to play, and it plays right through to the end.

The trigger can be something quite innocuous, such as a harmless joke or an unintentional reproach — someone says, "Your mother dresses you funny," or "Haven't you figured this out yet?" But to an individual, it may very well represent a lack of respect, a criticism, or a scolding. The behaviour pattern that results from this trigger, the same old song that our record plays, depends on how we have learned to respond over the years.

As children, we may have learned to get our way in a stressful situation by yelling and screaming and carrying on until people eventually backed down. Or we learned that if we cried, people would eventually feel sorry for us and give us what we wanted. If we whined, people would give up in frustration. By just remaining sullen, we could make other people feel guilty.

Changing these responses isn't perhaps as difficult as it may first appear. It really involves only two things: learning to recognize the triggers that get you started, and then disrupting the pattern, or "scratching" the record before we get too far into the song.

OUR EMOTIONAL TRIGGERS

We all have emotional triggers. Some of us have more than others, and they are different for each of us. Have you ever noticed, for example, how you can say one thing to one person and he will just laugh it off, yet saying the exact same thing to somebody else will trigger a full-scale explosion?

A friend of mine is a lawyer, and you can imagine how much abuse he puts up with under the guise of lawyer jokes. He laughs with the best of us and even manages to tell a few of his own. I met a lawyer just recently, however, for whom these jokes are no laughing matter. When somebody makes the mistake of telling a lawyer joke around him, he not only does not laugh, but he also launches into an angry monologue on the inappropriateness of this "humour."

The issue here isn't which one of these two lawyers has the right attitude. The issue is that for one of them, this is a trigger that sets off an emotional response. I make this point because we often ask ourselves why people are reacting in unexpected ways. "Why are they acting so unreasonably?" we wonder. Different people do react differently, but it doesn't necessarily mean they are being unreasonable. Just because somebody responds to different stimuli than you do doesn't mean that person is being unreasonable.

Identifying Your Triggers

Grab a piece of paper and a pen. If you don't have them handy, set the book down and go get them. Now, take a few minutes to think about what sets you off. Criticism? Threats? A lack of respect? Swearing? Suppression of your creativity? Somebody not listening to your point of view? People who speak loudly? There are as many different triggers as there are people. What are yours? Give some thought to it. Give some *real* thought to it. Think about the last time you got angry. What was it that got you going? What was it the other person said or did, or didn't say or do? Write down your triggers. Beside each one, write down why you think these triggers have an effect on you. What is it about your personality that has created these triggers?

This is a very difficult self-analysis project, but it is also a very important first step. It is unrealistic for you to expect that you will be able to manage your own emotional state if you don't have some idea of what it is that creates that emotional state. One of the amazing things about the human brain and human psychology is that we can begin mastering our own emotional state simply by identifying what our triggers are. We can begin rationalizing what once was just an automatic response.

Breaking the Pattern

Emotional states are progressive. Except in the rarest of situations, we don't instantly switch from contented to angry or sad to happy. From the initial trigger that sets us off, our emotions continue to build gradually within us, fuelled by our racing thoughts and our past experiences. And in confrontational situations, it's not just a matter of one person struggling with his ever-increasing emotional state. It's two or more people feeding off each other, creating even greater tension and anxiety.

Once I was flying back from Disney World with my wife, our three children, and my brother and sister-in-law. The first leg of our flight from Orlando to Newark had been delayed, which created a problem with our connection. We ran to the gate, only to discover that we had been given the wrong gate number. By the time we arrived at the right gate, our seats had been given to other passengers and we were informed that we'd been bumped to the next flight. That was, of course, if they could get us on the next flight, which was also overbooked.

The attendant at the gate was clearly having a stressful day. It was obvious that we weren't the first people to whom she had had to break bad news. I, too, was under some stress. After we arrived at our home airport, I still had to make a five-hour drive to get to another city for an 8 a.m. seminar the next morning. The confrontation started with three words: "We've been bumped?" I asked incredulously.

That was all it took for the gate attendant, who turned to me with fire in her eyes. "This wouldn't have happened if you had been here on time, sir!" came the scold.

You can imagine the effect *that* had on me. I very tersely explained my situation, and emphasized the fact that it was a foul-up on the part of her airline that caused us to be late. I then upped the emotional ante a little and suggested to her that the oversold seating was the airline's problem, not mine.

This, of course, pushed a couple of her own buttons. It was now her turn to crank up the heat a bit. Her voice got a little louder, she looked me in the eye, and stated very firmly, "No, sir, it is very much *your* problem. *You* are not on the airplane!"

My blood pressure went off the scale. I was ready for a fight, and she was going to be on the losing end. By the time this thing was through, I was determined to have seats on that airplane *and* her job.

Fortunately, I never got the chance to really work myself into a tizzy. My brother, who wasn't facing the same kind of time restraints I was, calmly stepped in and masterfully resolved the situation to everyone's benefit. With forty years of sibling experience behind him, he was able to recognize my emotional state and knew that things were only going to get worse.

What he did, essentially, was interrupt the emotional pattern he saw developing. He took the "I'm really mad, and I'm going to get you" record that had started to play in my mind and scratched it. He removed me from the situation just long enough for the emotional edge to disappear and the logical part of my brain to kick in.

Unfortunately, when we're faced with an emotional situation in our stores, we don't usually have a third party to rescue us. We're left to our own devices to change our own emotional state. That's why it is so important that we learn to understand the triggers that get us going, because the next step to controlling your emotional state is to start disrupting the learned behaviour pattern that follows. That is, you must find something that you can do yourself that will scratch the record you play in your brain, something that will interrupt the usual progression of emotions and behaviour.

To do this, you must learn to sharply redirect your focus. You must learn to give different meanings to the buttons that have been pushed in you so that they can be replaced by new, more productive responses. If, for example, you begin to feel defensive and start to get angry when someone says, "You don't know what you're talking about," you need to change that response to one that brings you confidence. If a person who shouts or uses foul language intimidates you, you need to change your reaction, perhaps to one of sympathy for someone who has poor interpersonal skills. In my case, the message I got from the airline person was "So what if you're the customer?" If I had tried, I could have turned my outrage into empathy by imagining the stress that gate attendant must have been under.

There are many different ways to break your initial emotional pattern. We've all seen the old routine in the movies where someone slaps a hysterical person in the face, and that person responds, "Thanks, I needed that!" As clichéd and campy as it seems, this is actually a classic pattern interrupter. It shifts the person's focus from the problem to his stinging cheek, and this instantly begins to generate a series of internal questions. What?! Why did he do that? What do I do now? As the focus changes, so does the person's behaviour.

Another classic pattern interrupter is the one recommended for people who become terrified at having to speak in public. You know, the old "picture everyone in the audience in their underwear" trick. Silly as it sounds, it works for many people.

But why does this underwear thing work? Well, think about the last time you had to give a speech. If you were nervous, the one big thought running through your mind was "Oh, God, I hope I don't screw up." The next thing you know, you're standing in front of the audience, shaking like a leaf. You're self-conscious and acutely aware of everything you say and how you say it. To your horror, you realize that you have tripped over a word or inadvertently missed part of your speech. Chances are your audience didn't notice, but you did, and your anxiety is now even greater. This increased anxiety causes you to make another error, which increases your anxiety even more, creating more errors, and so on. You're locked into a classic "anxiety-error-anxiety" spiral.

The "picturing people in their underwear" technique helps to break that spiral by briefly (and dramatically) shifting your concentration away from your own fears to your audience, long enough to give you a running start in the right direction. In theory, it allows you the opportunity to push the spiral upward instead of downward.

Think about this same process in terms of dealing with the Customer from Hell. The negative cycle may begin with a woman at the counter shouting, "I've been waiting for twenty minutes! Why the heck does it take you so long to do a simple price check?" The salesperson gets defensive and responds with a gentle scold: "I can't do anything about it, ma'am. It's a big store, you know." This irritates the customer even more, thus escalating the confrontation.

What if, in this situation, the salesperson had begun visualizing the customer standing there in her underwear? Would the reaction have been quite as defensive? I don't think so. It's hard to feel threatened by someone who shops in her underwear. I'm not suggesting, of course, that we shouldn't take our customers seriously. We should. It's just really important that we find ways to begin responding differently to their unpleasant behaviour.

Pattern-interruption techniques can be quite effective, but when the person is only a foot or two away from you and in your face, you may need to think of something a little more graphic. Instead of picturing your Customer from Hell standing there in her underwear, picture her standing there in a diaper. In your mind, stick a gigantic soother in her mouth. Put a huge blue bun like Marge Simpson's on the top of her head with a gigantic pink ribbon on top. Give female tormentors moustaches and male tormentors bras. You want something that is graphic enough, silly enough, and goofy enough to direct your focus away from your own needs and your own emotions, very much like a figurative slap in the face.

Of course, not all of us have the ability to visualize. But you can achieve the same pattern-interrupting result with a slight variation on the same technique. When I'm conducting workshops, I hand every participant a couple of blank pieces of paper and a box of crayons. The instructions are simple: draw a picture of the Customer from Hell. Make the most ridiculous, most fearsome customer you can possibly imagine. Give him two mouths. Have red smoke coming out of his nose and green stuff oozing from his ears. There is only one rule: you have to use every colour of crayon in the box to make the picture. I can tell you, I've had many a Serious Salesperson give me some pretty strange looks during this segment of the workshop.

Just for fun, put down this book again, grab another piece of paper and some crayons or coloured markers, and try it yourself. Oh, I know you'll feel silly, but try it anyway. If nothing else, you'll get to relive your childhood for a few moments. Once you've completed your picture, write the name LESTER under it. The reason for the name will become apparent as you read on in this book. If you just can't bring yourself to draw a picture, run down to the local shopping centre and put a couple of dollars in one of those mini-photo booths. Make weird faces. Make a rude hand gesture. Do something that's memorable. Give yourself something visual to work with. Now put LESTER someplace handy — under the cash counter, under a desk drawer, somewhere where he is easily accessible.

As soon as you realize you've come into contact with a difficult customer, as soon as you realize that your buttons are being pushed, as soon as you feel your emotions starting to swell, take a quick peek at your picture of LESTER. Then take a look at your customer. This may not appear to be a very sophisticated method of controlling your emotions, but I challenge you to do this exercise without experiencing a fairly significant shift in emotional state. Just a word of warning, however: laughing out loud or showing the picture to your customer is not recommended.

Here's another method. On yet another piece of paper, write down one word or phrase. It can be any word or phrase you like, but it has to be unusual, one you don't use regularly — something like "yikes," "wowee," "holy moly," or "Jiminy Cricket." Again, the way to apply it is simple: when you are faced with that very special customer, say that word in your mind (not out loud!) before you even open your mouth.

There are lots of other ways to interrupt your emotional state, but these are a few good ones. What you are trying to achieve, again, is brief but dramatic change to mental focus.

Keeping It Broke

These pattern-interruption techniques momentarily slow your behaviour pattern, which is the important first step. But what you really want to do is eliminate emotion from the equation and change the trigger permanently. You ultimately want to get to the stage where specific customer behaviour no longer lights your fuse to begin with. You do this by learning to ask yourself focusing questions.

Suppose you've just encountered a Customer from Hell who has suggested to you that you're lazy, which happens to be one of your hot buttons. You've used your picture of LESTER and momentarily gained control of your emotional state. What we *typically* do at this stage is start asking ourselves questions: "Who does he think he is, calling me lazy?" or "What can I do to prove to this guy that he's wrong?" Unfortunately, these questions don't solve anything. In fact, these are the very questions that make us angrier and add fuel to the fire.

What you need to do now is pose a whole new set of

questions: "Why is this customer so agitated?" "How am I going to resolve this problem?" "What's the real issue here?" This begins the process of focusing your thoughts on the *issue* instead of the emotions.

Underneath your picture of LESTER, write these three focusing questions:

1. Why is this customer so agitated?
2. What is the real issue?
3. How can we resolve this?

These are questions to ask of yourself, of course, *not* of your customer. Be aware that the answers to these questions are not always easily found. Although the answer may seem pretty obvious at times (for example, "This guy needs to return something that didn't work properly"), remember the five elements of expectations: need, situation, circumstance, personality, and predisposition. There is almost always more going on than is immediately obvious, and it requires a great deal of skill and more than a little patience to identify the whole reason for a customer's behaviour. If you truly concentrate on seeking the answers to these questions, if you make a real effort to better understand your customer, you'll be pleasantly surprised at the productive, constructive manner in which you will begin to approach problems.

For pattern interrupters and focusing questions to truly work, you have to make them work. You have to be committed to having them work. You have to learn to want to resolve the conflict. If you take the "what a jerk — I'll teach him for talking to me like that" attitude, then you might as well not even bother trying a pattern interrupter, because it won't work. If your focusing questions are negative — "What's this idiot's problem?" "What kind of personality disorder does he have?" "How can I shut him up?" — you will resolve nothing. The successful approach to the challenge of conflict always involves asking yourself, "How do we make this work to everyone's benefit?" instead of asking, "How can I win?"

Since you've already got that pen and paper handy, I'm going to ask you to do something else. Take a few moments to write down some specific instances when you have encountered a Customer from Hell. Try to record as many instances as you can. Put down as much detail as you can remember. Now take a look at that list and see if there are any similarities or trends. Do there tend to be any similar circumstances or situations involved? Does the conflict often involve a particular type of customer need? Are there specific (apparent) personality types involved when you find yourself in conflict? Do similar apparent predispositions appear to be present? If you spot any trends, write them down below your list. Make a commitment to yourself that the next time you find yourself in a similar situation, you will make a conscious effort to break your emotional pattern and ask yourself the three focusing questions.

All right now. You've come face to face with a Customer from Hell, successfully interrupted your emotional pattern, and asked yourself the focusing questions. It now becomes important that you maintain this little bit of control and keep yourself from starting to play that emotional record again. This requires you to concentrate and apply the techniques in the following chapter, as well as demonstrate a genuine desire to resolve the situation before it gets ugly.

The Good News

Here's the good news. After you've successfully used a pattern interrupter and the focusing questions over a period of time, you'll find yourself consciously using the techniques less and less often. Eventually, your brain will eliminate the middle man, and the trigger that used to set off a reactive emotional response will now automatically set off the questioning process. You will have begun to change your approach to conflict from a fight-or-flight response to a constructive resolution process.

Six months after I conducted a seminar on managing difficult situations, I received a letter from a saleswoman with an admitted short fuse. She wrote me to proclaim proudly that she hadn't had to look at her (very graphic) picture of LESTER in more than two months, and that she no longer "lost it" when a Customer from Hell popped by for a visit. "Now I just look at my LESTER picture when I'm fighting with my husband!" she said.

Into the Mouth of Hell

2

*There sighs, lamentations and loud wailing
resounded through the starless air, so
that at first it made me weep; strange
tongues, horrible language, words of pain,
tones of anger, voices loud and hoarse,
and with these the sound of hands, made
a tumult which is whirling through that air
forever dark, as sand eddies in a whirlwind.*

— DANTE'S INFERNO

Five

Introducing
LESTER

*The nifty part of the whole process
is that you don't have to wait for your
next Customer from Hell to show up
in order to practise it.*

LESTER is an acronym for the six steps to resolving the vast majority of difficult situations you will encounter in a retail or any other environment. The steps include:

- LISTENING to your customer;
- ECHOING the issue;
- SYMPATHIZING with your customer's emotional state;
- THANKING your customer for her input;

- EVALUATING your options;
- RESPONDING with a win-win solution.

This approach, which works better than any other conflict-resolution formula I have so far encountered, is based on one fundamental principle: the vast majority of difficult situations we encounter are the result of people who are *unsatisfied,* not people who are *unreasonable.* If we listen well enough to what these people have to say, the solutions to conflict become much more apparent. LESTER will help you quickly break through the elements of the situation that appear to be unreasonable, and will give you the ability to identify and resolve the causes of the dissatisfaction.

To make LESTER work for you, you must begin by accepting, at least for the time being, that nobody really wakes up in the morning and says, "By God, if I do nothing else today, I'm going to be a pain in the butt." You must believe that most people are like you and me. We have needs, our unique circumstances, our background situations, our own personalities, and our predispositions, all of which dictate our expectations. LESTER uses very specific techniques to help you focus on and identify these expectations, and thus deal with customers effectively.

LESTER is an intriguing concept once you've embraced it. As you practise and perfect it, you will begin to find that conflicts at work and at home are far less stressful. You will discover the true sense of satisfaction that comes from resolving conflict, instead of contributing to it.

Although I describe LESTER as a six-step process, it need not be either time-consuming or complex. Depending on the severity of the situation, it can be executed successfully in ninety seconds or nine minutes. In fact, the greatest challenge you will face is the same one we face when confronted with any new skill: the temptation to say, "I'm already doing all that!" None of the individual components of LESTER is likely to come as a massive revelation to you. I would suspect you're already using some of the skills, so you may find yourself feeling as if you know all this. But unless you're a whole lot different from the rest of us, you're not nearly as consistent, or as good at it, as you think you are.

The next chapters detail the six components of LESTER. If you are truly interested in mastering this process, I would suggest that you try to find some time to practise each component before you move on to the next. This will help you lock the process in your mind, and as a result will make it easier to remember when an opportunity to use it arises.

The nifty part of this whole process is that you don't have to wait for your next Customer from Hell to show up in order to practise it. It works at home as well as it does on the job, and it applies to everyday situations as well as conflict situations. And the best part is that learning to master your own emotional state and using the principles outlined in the next few chapters have very significant side-effects. These skills will also have a dramatic effect on how you are perceived by those customers in the store with whom you are *not* in conflict.

Let's say, for example, that you have a store full of people when, out of the blue, a customer gets in your face and starts shouting at you. "This is ridiculous! You call yourself a jeans store, but you never have my size in stock. I have asked and asked and asked, but you never get my size in stock. If you ask me, I think this is a pretty shoddy way of doing business!" This customer now has your full attention, as well as the attention of every other customer in the store. Like you, the other customers are uncomfortable, and for the most part, their instinctive response will be to sympathize with you. Their loyalties will change instantly, however, if you mishandle the situation. So you discreetly usher your customer off to a quiet corner of the store while you gain control of your emotions. You patiently and attentively listen, echoing the customer's points. You sympathize with his position, thank him very much for his input, make a determination as to what can be done, and respond to the situation. The customer walks away satisfied, believing that you do really care about him and his business.

What often will occur after this is that some of the other customers in the store will comment on how well you handled the situation. Many times I have had customers come up to me after I have managed an unpleasant situation and say, "Boy, I'm sure glad I wasn't in your shoes" or "It takes all kinds, doesn't it?" or "Isn't that awful? He had no right to talk to you like that."

When dealing with difficult situations, you must always be aware of the comfort level of the other customers in your store. You must be aware of this because there will come a time when you have to shift your focus from the needs of the Customer from Hell back to the needs of the other customers.

Six

......

Listening to Your Customer

....

Information is the key to understanding.
And the key to getting information is
improving our listening skills.

....

L istening. Sounds pretty basic so far, doesn't it? After all,
you're a good listener, aren't you? Heck, this chapter
should be a breeze. Well, before you skim through it and
move on, let's talk about what listening really is.

First of all, as you are no doubt aware, there is a dramatic
difference between listening and hearing. Hearing is physiological. Hearing is the body's response to sound waves.
Listening, on the other hand, is the translation of these sound
waves into meaning in the brain. Most of us can hear. Most

of us can listen. But it is *how* we listen that makes the difference between good listeners and poor listeners.

Listening is broken down by most experts into four levels. Without burdening you with a lot of detail, I can explain that someone who is listening at level four is simply not paying attention. The words are going in one ear and, as they say, out the other. A level-one listener, on the other hand, is somebody who has trained himself to listen. A level-one listener misses nothing. A level-one listener understands and appreciates all that he hears. Most of us fluctuate between level-two and level-three listening, which usually provides us with adequate information to complete our day-to-day tasks.

Have you ever been in the middle of a conversation with somebody and discovered to your horror that you haven't heard a word the person has said for the past fifteen seconds — and even worse, that she is awaiting your reply to some deep question she has asked? Or have you ever had a long conversation with somebody and discovered afterwards that the two of you were talking about two completely different things? Has anybody ever said to you, "That's not what I meant"? Has anybody ever said to you, "I just said that"? These are signs that we're not listening to the best of our capabilities, and it happens to all of us at some time or another. But there are good reasons for this: we are not born level-one listeners, and level-one listeners are not level-one listeners all of the time.

Try this simple game with a friend. Go to a new restaurant or some other unfamiliar place. Give your friend ten seconds to look around the room and memorize everything she can see that is white. Then ask her to close her eyes and name everything in the room that is green. She will recall very little, if anything. It's a tremendous demonstration that we have the capacity to remember and make meaningful only those things on which we focus.

Think for a moment about what the implications would be if we were able to concentrate completely on everything that we ever saw or heard. Imagine what it would be like to be able to recall at a moment's notice the tiniest detail. Take a look around you. How many different things can you see in the room you are sitting in now? The textures, the colours. What sounds can you hear right at this very moment? Now imagine if every little thing like this became committed to memory. Yikes!

To compensate for this information overload, our brains have been bestowed with a fairly complex filtering system. As information comes in through any of the five senses, your brain makes an instantaneous decision about whether to capture that information or let it go by. It then stores the selected information in your short-term memory and later on stores certain items in your long-term memory. What's interesting about this is that each of us has a unique set of filters. Have you ever noticed that some people can remember things you can't recall? Have you ever wondered how it is that somebody could forget something that you've remembered?

Some people, for example, have the wonderful ability to remember names and faces. And most of us are in awe of that salesperson who can remember the name of a customer who comes in only once a year. Other people have a knack for remembering phone numbers or what other people wear. We all have filters that we've developed over time.

Level-one listeners have trained themselves to remove most of their filters and absorb virtually everything for brief periods of time. This is an important skill because, as we will discover, information is the key to understanding. And the key to getting this kind of information is to improve our listening skills.

PARADIGM SHIFTS

Our beliefs and values all originate from the information we receive. As we learn more about people, places, and things — in other words, as our information changes — our beliefs and values begin to change accordingly. New information that challenges our beliefs is a part of all our lives. Think of some of the biggies: the earth is flat; man wasn't meant to fly; the earth is the centre of the universe; the Russians are the bad guys. We've all had to change our opinions at some point in our lives. After a while, the evidence becomes too great to ignore, and we are forced to re-evaluate some pretty fundamental beliefs.

When new information challenges, and ultimately changes, an existing belief, we experience what is called a paradigm shift. A paradigm shift is just a trendy five-dollar term that simply means a change in the rules, or a change in understanding. We experience paradigm shifts throughout our lives. For two days, you curse the manufacturer of your new television set because it hasn't worked all weekend, and then the repairman tells you it wasn't plugged in. You brag to your friends about your tough dog, Rambo, and then you discover "he" has given birth to a litter of pups. The guy you've always thought of as snooty turns out to be just painfully shy. Paradigm shifts can be mundane, or they can be quite dramatic.

In 1993, I was conducting a motivational customer-service seminar for a large group of retailers on the West Coast. I was about an hour into the program, right in the middle of a segment on the importance of smiling and body language. As you may expect, I like to get a little goofy and challenge the audience a bit. It's a lot of fun, and everybody gets a good laugh. Well, in this seminar, sitting right dead centre about five rows back, with her arms crossed and the biggest frown you can imagine, was a middle-aged woman named Verna. She stared and frowned and frumped at me to the point that it became unnerving. The unstated message, I thought, was quite clear: "I don't want to be here. I think you're stupid. I think the things you're saying are even more stupid. I refuse to laugh or smile, and there's nothing you can do that's going to make me."

I responded to this — as I do to most challenges — by getting even sillier, trying even harder to see if I could make her laugh. It became a mission, and yet was to no avail. The worst part was that I could see the people sitting around her becoming increasingly uncomfortable. This began to make me feel frustrated. "Couldn't this woman see the effect she was having on everybody else?" I wondered. "Couldn't she see that she was exuding the very behaviour I was trying to convince people to eliminate?" I had a break shortly after, and I couldn't get her out of my mind.

Apart from my personal frustration, I was concerned about the significant impact she was beginning to have on the rest of the audience. So I sat down for a few minutes to collect my thoughts and develop a strategy on how to deal with Verna. As I was sitting there, planning my approach, the district supervisor walked up to me with a big smile and said, "It looks like things are going pretty good!" I smiled back and said, "Yep, sure are. Good group. Sure is tough to make Verna smile, though."

The supervisor heaved a big sigh. "Verna," he said. "I can't even believe she's here. Eight days ago, her fourteen-year-old son was killed in a hit-and-run accident as he was walking to the hockey arena. The guy was drunk and ran right off the road onto the sidewalk. I tried to convince her to take some time off, but she's insisted on continuing to work."

Wow. Did I feel stupid, or what? My perspective on the situation changed instantly. Do you think I was still feeling frustrated? Quite the opposite, in fact. I was suddenly feeling pity, empathy, sympathy. It is a moment I will never, *ever* forget. *That* was a paradigm shift.

Imagine what might have happened had I not had the extreme good fortune to have the supervisor come in and give me that extra little bit of information. What do you suppose might have happened had I confronted her? Is it possible that, even if I had been light-hearted and gentle, I would have made the situation worse? I believe it was not only possible, but inevitable.

Have you ever been caught in this kind of situation? Have you ever become angered at something you thought a child, spouse, or co-worker had done, and then discovered later that they hadn't done it at all? These kinds of paradigm shifts occur often and affect us throughout our lives.

So what's the lesson here? The more information we have before we act, the greater our chances for success and the less likely we'll be taken by surprise. This holds true for virtually every aspect of life, and dealing with the Customer from Hell is no different. The more information, the better — and that's what listening is all about.

THE PRINCIPLES OF LISTENING

The most common and most devastating mistake people make when faced with a Customer from Hell is to try to resolve the problem before really understanding what it is.

There are four fundamental principles of effective listening. As we go through these principles, each one will likely appear to you to be common sense. But as my father used to say, "The problem with common sense is that it ain't so common."

There are two things that we are trying to accomplish by listening. First, we are trying to get as much information as possible. We need to learn as much as we possibly can about the needs, situations, circumstances, personalities, and predispositions that make up our customers' expectations. That, perhaps, is obvious. The second goal, however, is less obvious. By listening carefully, we are trying to communicate to our customers (some of whom may very well be agitated) that we do, in fact, care about them and their situation.

Why do we need to communicate that we care? Well, I believe that if there is one thing that all Customers from Hell have in common, it is that they think you don't care. They think that you (either personally or corporately) are the bad guy. They perceive the interaction as a "me versus you" confrontation. It makes sense to me that if a customer believes that you genuinely care about her problem, she will be a lot more pleasant.

If we've already managed to get some control over our own emotional state, our goal now becomes to try to help our difficult customers gain control over their emotional states. Right now, they've got something to get off their chests. Being aware of, and implementing, the four principles of effective listening will go a long way to helping you defuse a customer's volatile emotional state.

Principle #1: Undivided Attention

The first and most basic principle of listening is to give the other person your undivided attention. What does this mean? Well, it means putting down your clipboard. It means turning to face her. It means setting aside any other tasks that you are working on. It means not working the cash register when you are speaking with her. It means — get this — *not talking!*

Have you ever tried to talk to someone when you weren't quite sure he or she was paying attention? It's a little frustrating, isn't it? You start to get the feeling that the person doesn't really care, and that your message is not getting through. Now put the shoe on the other foot and imagine how that feeling might affect an upset customer. Giving your customers your undivided attention is a critical first step towards communicating to them that you are on their side. Hear them out. Let them know you care.

When you are confronted with an unpleasant situation, it is always a good idea to try, whenever possible, to lead your customer to a quiet, out-of-the-way spot in the store. As well as minimizing the disruption to the rest of the customers and staff, this also takes you away from any distractions. It sets you up for success.

Leading the customer away from the initial point of confrontation requires a little finesse, however. He may think that you're trying to shuffle him aside, or that you are afraid of being embarrassed, which will only worsen his emotional state. Present the move as a positive. Let the customer know that you believe his concerns to be important and that you want to hear him out without any distractions.

For example, instead of saying, "Let's go over here to talk about this," try saying, "This is important to me, sir. Why don't we find a quieter spot so I can give you my undivided attention?" Wording your request this way serves to remove both you and your customer from everyone else, and also establishes that you consider him an important customer, and that you are interested in what he has to say.

Sometimes, of course, the customer may insist on staying where he is. If that is the case, you'll have to go with the flow and deal with him on the spot. Whatever you do, *don't* try to move him again. It will only make things worse.

Principle #2: Eye Contact/Body Language

The second principle of effective listening involves eye contact and body language. There is nothing more unnerving than trying to have a conversation with someone who won't look at you or whose eyes seem to wander while you're talking to her. Have you ever had a conversation with some-body who is slumped over in his chair, his back slightly turned to you? The message that comes across is loud and clear: "I don't care, I don't want to be here, and I don't really want to be listening to this." That, of course, may not be the case at all. It is, however, the way we perceive body language.

Many, many years ago (back when I had a real job), I worked as an account manager in an international advertising agency. One of the most instructive lessons of my early career occurred when a vice-president walked into my office one sunny morning and dropped a videotape on my desk. "Watch this," he said, "then report to boardroom B at three o'clock." And with that, he turned and strolled out.

I found myself an empty room with a video player, plugged in the tape, and sat down. To my great distress, I discovered that the featured topic was *me*. An hour and a half of *me*. They had set up a camera behind one-way glass in one of the boardrooms and videotaped my meetings and presentations to clients. They had done this with all of my colleagues as well, and the purpose was to prepare us for a training session on presentation skills. The tape was excruciating to watch. My body language was awful: I slouched, I shuffled, my arms flailed, my head bobbed around. It was then that I realized how critical body language is in the communication process.

When you are in a difficult situation with a customer, be very conscious of the subtle yet powerful messages you are sending with your body. Don't cross your arms. If you do, you will be perceived as unreceptive. Don't slouch or lean on something — your customer will think you don't care. Don't cock your hip. If you do, you'll look impatient.

Here are some basic rules of body language:

1. *Stand up straight.*

Okay, so you heard this a hundred times from your mother — but it's still true. If you slouch, shuffle, or keep your head down, you will be perceived as uninterested and ineffective. You simply won't be able to create any kind of connection with your customer.

Keep your arms by your sides or fold your hands (not your arms) in front of you. I suggest you avoid clasping your hands behind your back in the traditional military "at ease" position. This can come across as "I'm listening to you not because I want to, but because I have to."

If you happen to be sitting down, don't lean back. Don't put your feet up or cross your legs. Lean forward and put your forearms on your knees or on the table.

2. *Don't square your shoulders to your customer.*

Be careful about how you stand facing your customer. If your shoulders are square to your customer — that is, so that you are directly face to face — you are in a confrontational position.

The next time you're talking with someone in normal circumstances, take a close look at how you stand. You'll notice that your feet and the feet of the person you are talking to are not directly in front of each other, but instead are very slightly angled. When you are face to face with an agitated customer, make sure that your stance is similar. Of course, you also want to make sure that you are not standing at too great an angle. You don't want to give the impression that you would rather be looking somewhere else.

3. *Keep your best poker face.*

In the critical first few moments of a difficult situation, a raised eyebrow, a smile, a frown, even a twitch can be misinterpreted.

4. *Stand still.*

Try not to shift your weight back and forth. This could be perceived as impatience.

5. *Look into your customer's eyes.*

You need to send the message loud and clear that this customer, at this moment in time, is the most important person in your life. I'm not suggesting that you stare at your customer, engaging him in a "who blinks first" contest. But make sure that you are making eye contact, especially when your customer is clearly agitated.

6. *Eliminate the barriers.*

I touched on this when I talked about the importance of giving customers your undivided attention. Barriers such as clipboards, pricing guns, and inventory stand in the way of creating the atmosphere of trust that is so crucial at this stage. If you are standing behind a counter, move out from behind it. If you are seated at a desk, move so that the desk is no longer between you and your customer.

These barriers — the desks, clipboards, etc. — silently reinforce the "me versus them" feelings your customer may already have. To build trust, you must be prepared to create a level of intimacy that encourages your customer to perceive you as a person rather than just a representative of the company.

Our own body language is as difficult to recognize as it is to change, mainly because the ways we move and stand are pure habit. But the process of becoming aware of our body language in stressful situations can be extremely useful. It's kind of like the pattern-interruption techniques I talked about earlier. The more you focus on your body language, the less you will be able to focus on your emotional state.

Principle #3: Prompt

The third principle of effective listening is prompting. Prompting is the technique we use for encouraging people to continue talking. We all do it to some degree, but for most of us it is a haphazard, instinctive thing. We grunt and mumble at each other to fill the silence, but we don't often give much thought to the real purpose of prompting or how to do it skilfully.

When we have an unpleasant situation, we *want* our customers to talk. We want them to tell us as much as they can. We have to actively encourage them to communicate with us at every opportunity, even if what they are saying is hard to listen to. The most common and most devastating mistake people make when faced with a Customer from Hell is to try to resolve the problem before really understanding what it is. For most of us, our instinctive response when confronted with conflict is to try to remove ourselves from the situation as quickly as possible. Because of this, we more often than not attempt to resolve the conflict before we have adequate information. We respond *too quickly*.

The results of responding prematurely are never positive,

and yet in virtually all Customer from Hell encounters that's exactly what we do. Take this potentially difficult situation:

Customer: Do you work here?

Salesperson: Yes, sir.

Customer: Well, I want to know where the hell my widget is, and I want to know *now!*

Salesperson: Which widget is that, sir?

Customer: The one you people said would be in three weeks ago!

Salesperson: May I have your name, sir?

Customer: Smith. Bob Smith. I've been in here three times, and each time someone tells me, "It should be here in a week."

Salesperson: Let me just check on that, sir. [*Retreats to the back room for a couple of minutes, then returns.*] It still hasn't arrived, Mr. Smith. I'm not sure what the hold-up is, but it should be here any day.

Customer: [*Yelling.*] And so should Christmas! I tell you what — you can take your order and shove it where the sun don't shine! I am sick and tired of this useless store! You don't give a damn about me or my business!

Salesperson: Well, we really don't have any control over our suppliers —

Customer: That's your problem, not mine! Maybe they don't like you either! [*Stomps out.*]

Why did the customer walk out? Was it really all the fault

of the supplier? Was it just an ill-tempered customer? I don't think so. The seed of discontent perhaps originated with the supplier, and the customer was certainly agitated, but the stressful situation was created by the salesperson's not dealing with the real issue. What was the real issue? Well, let's run the example again, this time a little differently, and find out:

Customer: Do you work here?

Salesperson: Yes, sir.

Customer: Well, I want to know where the hell my widget is, and I want to know *now!*

Salesperson: Your widget, sir?

Customer: The one you people said would be in three weeks ago!

Salesperson: Oh no.

Customer: Oh, yes! You people keep telling me, "It should be here in a week," and I've come in three times now!

Salesperson: Really?

Customer: You bet. And I tell you it's frustrating. I have to drive twenty-five miles to get to your store!

Salesperson: Twenty-five miles?

Customer: [*A little quieter.*] I need this widget in a bad way.

Salesperson: It sure sounds like it.

Customer: Well, without it, my new business is never going to get off the ground.

Salesperson: Oh dear.

Customer: Yes, sir. And the hour and a half of driving back and forth to this store isn't helping. Every minute I'm out of the office costs me money . . .

In this example, we've now learned that while the problem may be the supplier's tardiness, the issue is the disruption to the man's business. We're also in a better position to understand why he is agitated. We haven't solved the problem yet, but our options for solutions — such as delivery or a direct-from-supplier shipment — are now increasing.

The difference in the second example was that the salesperson prompted the customer with words and phrases like "oh no," "really," "oh dear," etc. Effective prompting is accomplished with such single words or brief phrases that express interest. It encourages people to talk more, reiterate points, and clarify issues.

Effective prompting achieves two very important objectives. First, it provides you with more information — in this case, we learned about the new business, the long drive, and the financial implications. Second, it gives your customer a chance to wind down and get better control of his emotions.

Perhaps the most common, and unfortunately the least productive, ways of prompting are with the old favourites "uh-huh" and "mm-hmm." When you say "uh-huh" or "mm-hmm" to someone, you are sending that person a clear message that you are not terribly interested and that you aren't really paying attention. It's a habit that neither requires nor stimulates thought. Unfortunately, it is also one of the toughest habits in the world to break. But if you can stop grunting at the people you're supposed to be listening to, you'll be amazed at how much your listening will improve.

The practice of prompting is a useful asset not only when dealing with difficult customers but also in everyday life. The next time you are having a discussion with your spouse, child, or co-worker, practise this technique. Let them do the talking. See how much information you can get out of them with the simple words and phrases like "oh" and "really" and "is that right?"

Here's an example. My eleven-year-old daughter came home from school one day to tell me that her teacher had unfairly and undeservedly punished her entire class.

"Really?" I said, trying not to sound incredulous.

"Yeah, and we hadn't done anything at all!" my daughter continued.

"Is that right?" I prompted.

"Yeah. All we were doing was talking about the assignment, and she just started yelling!"

"No kidding?"

"I mean" — my daughter looked down a bit — "she told us yesterday that she didn't want any talking in the class, but we just forgot."

"You forgot," I said gently.

"Well, I guess she had a right to be upset, but we didn't do it on purpose."

Case closed.

What makes prompting so difficult when dealing with unpleasant customers is that they are so . . . well, unpleasant. We don't really want to listen to any more abuse. It goes against our nature to do anything to encourage unpleasantness. The hidden trap, however, is that if we fail to prompt, if we fail to extract all the additional and necessary information we can, we risk making unpleasant behaviour worse.

One word of caution with prompting: be very careful of your tone of voice. You want to sound inquisitive and interested, not challenging or sarcastic.

Principle #4: Visualize

The fourth principle of effective listening is to visualize. Try to get a picture in your mind of what the person is saying. Try to understand why she is feeling the way she is. How would you react in that situation if you were in her shoes? If you can visualize the expectations of the customer, your understanding of the situation will increase. You will also find that your own emotional state will start to improve. It becomes increasingly difficult to stay upset with somebody when you are standing in her shoes.

If you do nothing other than learn to skilfully apply these four principles of listening when difficult situations arise, a curious thing will happen: almost half of these potentially explosive situations will simply evaporate. They will resolve themselves with very little further input on your part. This happens for a few reasons. For starters, if you have truly spent all that time listening, you haven't had the opportunity to stick your foot in your mouth, to say something that might make the situation worse. (Remember the old saying "A closed mouth gathers no foot.") Second, if the customer did come in spoiling for a fight, she didn't get one. And third, quite often the complaining customer simply wants to be heard.

BARRIERS TO LISTENING

Listen a hundred times.
Ponder a thousand times.
Speak but once.
— TURKISH PROVERB

Shut Up!

The barriers to effective listening are many, and most are exceedingly difficult to overcome. Perhaps the greatest one of these is our temptation to talk.

For many of us, the biggest challenge in life is keeping our mouths shut long enough to actually hear what other people are saying. When we're not talking, we're planning what we're going to say next. These are habits we've developed over a lifetime, and ones that are very difficult to break. But break them we must if we want to have any hope of successfully resolving conflict.

Here's a great exercise. The next time you're out at a social function, try not to speak unless you are asked a direct question. Don't be rude, of course. Keep smiling and making eye contact, but just don't talk. Time yourself to see how well you're doing. In addition to being wonderful practice for the next time you're face to face with a Customer from Hell, this exercise will also have people around you thinking you're poised, confident, and contemplative.

One time I was on a sales call, meeting with the director of marketing of a large super-regional shopping centre. I introduced myself, allowed myself two or three very brief sentences on who we were and what we did, then said, "So, tell me about the mall!" The meeting lasted almost two hours, and I didn't utter another full sentence. She told me story after story of every marketing program they had run for the past twenty years. She told me of all the celebrities she had met, and of her numerous successes and awards. She told me how she liked to travel to Las Vegas three or four times a year. She talked of her children, grandchildren, cousins, nieces, and nephews. I knew more about this marketing director by the end of the meeting than I knew about myself.

As I was getting up to leave, I offered to send her a reference list of other clients for whom we had worked. She pushed at the air with her hands and said, "I don't need any references! I can tell just from our conversation that you can do the job. Let's plan to start May 15." Silence truly is golden.

Be Aware of Your Own Stress Level

Another great barrier to effective listening is your own stress level. It is tough to devote yourself to other people's problems when you're living with problems of your own. Stresses in business and in your personal life can be distracting at best, and in an often frenzied retail environment, the challenge to overcome them is magnified dramatically.

Be aware of your own emotional state. If you find yourself getting a little overwhelmed, take a short break or even a day off. You're not doing yourself or anyone else any favours by showing up for work when you're not at your best.

I'll just say one last thing about improving your skills. Simply reading about listening in this book won't help you. Please don't believe for a second that understanding the concepts alone will make you a better listener. You must practise and practise diligently. Practise the skills at home and in non-conflict situations. Practise them at work. Practise them whenever and wherever you can. Make listening a part of your life.

Here again are the basics:

- *Undivided attention.* Drop what you're doing and concentrate on your customer.
- *Eye contact/body language.* Let your customer know you care.
- *Prompt.* Encourage him to keep talking.
- *Visualize.* Put yourself in her shoes.

Seven

Echoing
the Issue

Let the customers have their say,
make sure you understand exactly
what it is they are saying,
and let them know you've heard it.

A fascinating thing often happens when we're in a confrontation: we repeat ourselves. We make our points
again and again, a little louder each time. We reiterate,
re-emphasize, restate. We do this because we're convinced
that our point isn't getting across, that the other person isn't
really listening. "You just don't get it!" we scream silently.

This is where echoing comes in. Echoing is actually part of
the listening process, but I separate it out here because it's
quite a distinctive skill and one that merits some discussion.

Echoing, or reflective listening, is the process by which we feed back to the customer what he or she perceives to be the key issue.

Take this customer in a women's fashion store, for example. "The salesperson I bought this blouse from three weeks ago promised me that it wouldn't shrink if I washed it in the washing machine," she complains. "Well, look at it! It must be a whole size smaller! There's no way I can wear it any more. Why don't you people get the information straight on the products you sell?" The salesperson, echoing, would respond with something like, "It's a whole size smaller?"

Echoing is the process of taking a statement made by a customer and repeating the *issue* back to that customer as close to word for word as possible. This accomplishes three things. First, and most important, it lets your customer know that you are, in fact, listening. There will be no need for her to repeat herself. This helps reduce the tension and helps the customer gain some control of her emotional state, allowing both customer and salesperson to move forward in the resolution process.

Second, echoing confirms your understanding; it makes sure that you are both talking about the same thing. By doing this, you reduce the risk of miscommunicating and making the situation worse. And third, echoing helps you and your customer concentrate on the issue instead of on the emotions. You will find yourself less prone to feeling personally attacked.

When you've echoed properly, the Customer from Hell has two basic responses open to him: "Yes, that's right" or "That's not what I said (or meant)." If he responds with

"Yes, that's right," you've reassured him that you do, in fact, understand the problem. If he responds with "No, that's not what I meant," then you have prevented a potential miscommunication.

Effective echoing requires some skill. If you don't do it properly, it can backfire on you. Following are three fundamental rules for echoing.

ECHO THE ISSUE, NOT THE EMOTION

As you are listening, the customer will be communicating many things to you. He will be communicating his emotional state, his sense of frustration, his anger, his outrage, possibly his sense of betrayal or his sense of helplessness. He will also be telling you what the problem is and the situation surrounding it.

In the example I gave at the beginning of the chapter, the *issue* was that the blouse was a whole size smaller. One of the *emotional* comments from the customer, however, was "Why don't you people get the information straight on the products you sell?" The customer had clearly put her faith in the salesperson and her knowledge of her products, and she was feeling betrayed.

As you listen, you will get some glimpses of your customer's needs, situation, circumstances, personality, and predispositions. It's entirely possible that your customer will talk, bellow, scream, or rant for three or four minutes. Large chunks of what you hear will be manifestations of the emotional baggage the customer has brought in with him. It is not as easy as it may first appear to separate the real issue from all the rest of the information you are receiving. But if you don't, your echoing can lead to disaster.

Let's take another look at our example. What if the salesperson had echoed, "There's no way you could wear it?" What is the message the customer might get from this? It's possible the customer may have interpreted this as "So what if it shrank a bit? Of course you can still wear it." Or she might have heard, "Why don't you wear it anyway?" This would lead only to an escalation of her emotional state. You see, when a customer says, "There is no way I can wear it now," she is expressing her sense of frustration. The problem is that the product shrank. The effect of that problem on the customer is that she can no longer wear the blouse.

What if the salesperson had echoed, "You want to know why we don't learn more about our products?" The customer would likely hear that as a challenge. It would sound to her defensive or argumentative. The customer would then feel the need to defend her statement. Remember, when a customer says something like "Why don't you people get the information straight on the products you sell?" she is expressing her sense of frustration that she put her trust in the salesperson and that salesperson let her down. She had positive expectations of the salesperson's ability and she was, in her mind, betrayed.

Isolating the real issue to echo is a far greater challenge than it appears at first. You may not grasp the magnitude of the difficulty until you are actually in a conflict situation. A person may be screaming at you, bellowing, whining, or crying. She may be extremely confrontational, making you feel defensive. In those circumstances, it is very difficult to remain detached and logical. But the pleasant side-effect of learning how to pierce through all of the miscellaneous information and concentrate on the key issue is that it does help you keep your own emotional equilibrium. You are focusing more on what the actual problem is and less on the hot buttons that this customer is pushing.

Here are a couple of examples of things disgruntled customers might say. See how quickly you can determine the real issue.

EXAMPLE #1: NOTHING TO WEAR

"Honestly, I don't know why I even bother to shop in this store. This happens to me every single time! I'm telling you, the dress is a full inch longer than it should be. Who the heck does your alterations, anyway? I need it fixed, and I need it fixed now! I can't wait another day. It has been five days already . . . far too long, if you ask me. I bought this dress specifically for a wedding I'm attending tomorrow, and there's no way I'm going to wear it like this. I paid you people a lot of money for this dress, and I expect it to be altered properly. It's at least twenty dollars less at the store just down the street, but I bought it here expecting some service. I guess I was wrong!"

What is the issue here? Quite simply, it is that the dress a customer has purchased in your store to wear to a wedding is too long. Several of her statements — "This always happens," "Who does your alterations?" "I paid too much," and "You're too slow" — are simply expressions of her frustration. It would be a huge mistake (and an easy one) to fall into the trap of addressing any one of them.

The proper way to echo the issue back to the customer in this situation would go something like this: "The dress you need for a wedding tomorrow is too long?" Nice and simple, non-confrontational, and no finger-pointing. You could say, "The dress you need for a wedding tomorrow wasn't altered properly?" but then you might be setting yourself up for unwarranted blame. It could be possible that the alterations were perfect, but customer wore different shoes when the clothes were marked. When echoing an issue, you must try to be as neutral as possible.

EXAMPLE #2: THE HORRIFIED HOST
"This meat is rancid! I have never been so embarrassed in my life. Here I was preparing for a dinner party, only to find that the main course was going to be ruined. I have half a mind to call the health department on you people. Have you no quality control? I can't believe you thought that you could get away with selling this. Do you think I'm stupid? My God, it's just fortunate that I've caught it in time, before I made all my guests sick."

What's going on in the second example? Is the issue one of quality control? Her threat to call the health department? That she thought you were trying to "get away with something"? Should you echo, "You've got half a mind?" No. The issue is that the meat she bought for an important dinner party was bad. And that's exactly how to echo it: "The meat you bought here to serve at a dinner party was bad?"

The customers in each example had a right to feel frustrated. Regardless of who was to blame in either case, they still had a right to feel frustrated. Echoing lets them know, without challenging them on the specifics of what happened, that you understand precisely why they are frustrated.

WATCH YOUR TONE OF VOICE

We've all heard the old phrase "It's not what you say, but the way you say it." Goodness knows, you'll see me refer to it more than once in this book. And nowhere is this phrase truer than in the case of echoing. Even when you're echoing the proper issue, the process will be counterproductive if the customer detects sarcasm, disbelief, surprise, or anger in your voice.

Think again of the example at the beginning of the chapter. The proper response for the salesperson was "It's a whole size smaller?" Just for fun, say that out loud. Say it with a really sarcastic tone of voice, then say it with disbelief. Now say it again with an angry tone of voice. Can you hear the difference? Can you see the effect your tone of voice would have on someone?

Let's take this exercise one step further, just to make a point. Repeat this sentence out loud: "That car is red."

On the whole, a pretty bland statement. Now use the exact same sentence to

- express disgust over the colour;
- express surprise over the colour;
- express disgust about the car;
- express great happiness over the colour;
- express indifference over the colour;

- make a point of the colour to someone for the third time.

Remarkable, isn't it? Tone of voice plays an enormous role in our society. When echoing, your tone is critical. For echoing to work, your customer must get the message clearly that you are listening and that you care.

DON'T GET DEFENSIVE

Another common mistake we make in conflict situations is to get defensive or start providing explanations. Although providing an explanation may be valuable or necessary at some point, this is not the time to do it. Remember that what we want to do is let the customers have their say, make sure we understand exactly what it is they are saying, and let them know we've heard it. As a rule of thumb, never try to "explain" things to an agitated customer unless absolutely necessary. You will only be perceived as making excuses.

Perhaps the next worst thing you can do is to try to pass the blame back to the customer. If, in the example of the customer with the shrunken blouse, the salesperson had replied, "Well, what temperature did you wash it in?" the customer would only have got defensive, adding fuel to the confrontation.

> Always ask yourself what is more important —
> ending a war or winning a war.

When I'm conducting seminars on dealing with the Customer from Hell, I will occasionally, at this point, start getting "yabuts" (yeah, but . . .). "Yabut, what if it is the customer's fault?" someone will ask me. "Am I just supposed to let them get away with being rude?" Or "Yabut sometimes the customer is just being totally stupid!"

No, you don't have to let your customer get away with being rude, and yes, sometimes customers are being totally stupid. You are well within your rights to stand up for yourself and "straighten the customer out." But here's a question: What is more important — ending a war or winning a war? There's no right answer; it's a personal choice. But if, deep down, winning conflict is more important to you than ending conflict, programs such as this will never work for you. And you will always find yourself with more than your share of conflict.

At the echoing stage, you may very well find yourself biting your tongue an awful lot, but if you are interested in ending the war, it's worth it. It is difficult to put into words the kind of effect that echoing can have on someone. You really have to try it and see for yourself. The changes in the other person's body language and attitude can be quite dramatic as the message — "She heard me, and she understands" — sinks in.

....

EIGHT

Sympathizing with Your Customer

....

*It is critical that your customer
stop perceving you as an opponent
and start perceiving you as an ally.*

....

In the listening and echoing processes, we have begun to break down some of the barriers between you and the customer. The customer is beginning to believe that maybe you do care, and the seeds of trust have been sown. You will find that by the time we've reached this stage (which, by the way, may take only a minute or two), the edge is off the customer's voice. The intensity has diminished considerably. We are still in conflict, but we are less and less in confrontation.

The next step is to reinforce and solidify the perception that you care. William Ury, in his book *Getting Past No*, refers to this process as "stepping to their side." It's a wonderful metaphor for the transition from confrontation to mutual problem-solving that takes place during conflict. But for this transition to take place, it is critical that your customer stop perceiving you as an opponent and start perceiving you as an ally. And the best way to accomplish this is by letting her know that you understand her situation and that you sympathize with what she is going through.

The operative word here is "sympathize," not "agree," and I can't make that point strongly enough. You do not have to agree with somebody's point of view to sympathize with how she is feeling. Try saying something simple, such as, "From what you've told me, I can understand how you'd feel that way." In saying this, you are conveying to the person that you understand her emotions. You aren't agreeing with her position or her opinions, but you are recognizing her emotional state and her right to feel that way.

If you have truly listened to what your customer has to say, echoed the key issue back to her, and put yourself in her shoes, sympathizing isn't as difficult as you may believe. Remember my experience with Verna? Even the best of us, given a strong enough need, a desperate situation, and a negative predisposition, can behave badly.

I should also stress that sympathizing does not mean apologizing. Apologizing, when required, is part of the final step of LESTER, the response. But there are times when apologizing is neither necessary nor appropriate. Be careful that you don't say, "I'm sorry that this happened to you," or "I'm sorry we messed up," or "I'm sorry that you feel that way." We don't want to apologize at this stage. What we do want to do is express understanding.

Take a look again at the words I used above: "From what you've told me, I can understand how you'd feel that way." What are the customer's options for a response to this statement? She may say, "Well, I hope so," or "I'm sure you do," or "So what are you going to do about it?" Or she may just break down and cry. (I've seen it happen more than once.) However she responds, I guarantee it will be far less confrontational than when you first saw her. If she does say, "So what are you going to do about it?" that's terrific. She is sending you the message that she's got everything off her chest and is ready to begin resolving the problem.

One of my companies is RetailTrack, a national mystery-shopping service. We have a network of hundreds of investigators across the country who discreetly visit our clients' stores and provide an assessment of their customer-service levels. Occasionally, a store does not score very well, and some store managers can become quite defensive. Once I was speaking to a group of about 200 store managers, introducing the overall results of a recent shop. One manager in the group was quite distressed over what she felt was a grossly unfair score, and she raised her hand to tell me so. I was faced with the same two options you are faced with in your store: Do I address the problem right here and now, in a public forum, or try to find a more suitable venue for the discussion?

I told her that this was an issue I took quite seriously, that the integrity of the program was paramount, and that therefore her concerns were very important to me indeed. I suggested to her that we speak together about it at the upcoming break. She agreed.

To say that she was not very pleasant to listen to was an understatement. She was bitter and angry, and extremely vocal. It turned out that she had received the lowest score in the chain, and that the three employees on duty that day were all brand new and not yet up to speed. "How am I supposed to motivate these people with you telling them that they are the bottom of the barrel?" she snorted.

As I patiently listened and prompted and echoed, I discovered that the employees were hired to replace three people who had left, with very little notice, to go to school. As a last resort, she had hired three of her daughter's best friends. They weren't working out at all, it seemed, but the manager couldn't discipline them or let them go without running the risk of alienating her daughter.

This was a manager who had made a fundamental mistake in her hiring practices, and she knew it. Every bone in my body was screaming, "It's not *our* fault you hired the wrong people!" But with a great deal of effort, I decided to practise what I preach instead. "From what you've told me, I sure can understand your frustration," I said softly. Her voice dropped so low I could barely hear it. She began to cry. "I just don't know how to get out of this mess, and now, with this score, my supervisor thinks I'm a terrible manager." To make a long story short, we were able not only to eliminate the conflict but also to resolve her employee problem that day, and I gained a lifelong friend.

So let's take a look now at how the first three stages of LESTER work. We'll start with an example of a typical Customer from Hell experience:

Customer: "I hate having to shop in this store! I wouldn't, you know, if it wasn't that my son is desperate for this toy and you're the only ones in this end of the city who sell it!"

Salesperson: [*Uneasy silence*]

Customer: "You people don't even care. You don't care about your customers. All you care about is making a quick buck from this junk you sell!"

Salesperson: "We care very much about our customers, ma'am."

Customer: "You do not! You sell defective merchandise, which I'm constantly bringing back for refunds; your prices are way higher than every place else in the city; and the people working here are *rude!*"

Salesperson: "I'm sorry, ma'am, but we really have no control over our suppliers' quality. We do, however, give refunds when there is a problem. And our prices are quite competitive."

Customer: "Young lady, don't try to tell me about prices! Do you not think I shop around? I do, you know. And I don't need some part-time clerk to tell me that I don't know what I'm talking about!"

Salesperson: [*Giving up in frustration*] "Ma'am, I don't set the prices. I'm afraid you'll have to talk to my manager about that."

Customer: "Like the manager's going to do something about it! All you people do is rip off people like me. It's all right, though — you'll learn your lesson when you go out of business."

Salesperson: "Well, we've been around for twelve years. I hardly think —"

Customer: "I don't have time to argue with another rude clerk in this store. Just forget it. And forget about this toy. I'll go across town and get it." [*Customer stomps off.*]

Salesperson: What's her problem?"

Let's see how the same scenario might have played out had the salesperson followed the first three steps of LESTER:

Customer: "God, I hate having to shop in this store! I wouldn't, you know, if it wasn't for the fact that my son is desperate for this toy and you're the only ones in this end of the city who sell it."

Salesperson: [*Prompting*] "Really?"

Customer: "Yes 'really.' I don't think I've ever bought a thing in this store that I wasn't disappointed with — and the people here are really rude."

Salesperson: [*Prompting*] "Oh, no . . ."

Customer: "Yes. Sometimes I just want to scream. I don't mind paying the higher prices if I'm treated well, but I'm not. Half the time I'm just ignored."

Salesperson: [*Echoing*] "You've been ignored?"

Customer: "More times than I can count. And I just don't have the time to stand about waiting for someone to get around to me."

Salesperson: [*Sympathizing*] "From what you've told me, I sure can understand how you'd feel frustrated."

Customer: "Frustrated isn't the word. In the past two months, my son has broken three toys and I've had to bring them back. I was really made to feel like I was a big pain in the you-know-what."

Salesperson: [*Echoing*] "You've had toys break?"

Customer: "I know it's not your fault — you don't make them — but . . ."

Do you see the change in the customer's attitude? The problem's not solved yet, but the confrontation is gone. We've learned that the real issue isn't price or the defective merchandise, it's that the customer feels neglected and uncomfortable, and that's what's causing the conflict. But we had to actively listen to learn this.

Although I am presenting LESTER in a logical sequence, you'll notice that the listening and echoing activities continue throughout the process. Now you know why we spend so much time on these two elements. They are the essence of conflict resolution.

Nine

Thanking Your Customer

The package that complaints come in is ugly, grotesque, and unpleasant, yet what is inside is of critical importance to you and your business.

As odd as it may seem, the pivotal point of turning confrontation into active problem solving is usually when you get around to thanking your customer. "Let me get this straight," you're probably saying to yourself. "I'm supposed to take this person who has been bellowing at me for the past five minutes and *thank* him?" Well, yes. "Do I really have a reason to thank him?" you may ask. Again, the answer is a resounding yes.

Here's a question for you. When most customers become dissatisfied with you or your products, whom do they tell? You? No way. They tell everyone *but* you. They tell their friends, acquaintances, business associates, sometimes even total strangers. At best, maybe two of every hundred dissatisfied customers actually take the time and have the inclination, the energy, and the desire, or care enough about you and your business, to lodge a complaint with you or your company.

Think about it from your own perspective. When was the last time you wrote a letter to a manager? When was the last time you went into a store to express your discontent over something? We just don't do it very often. The problem is, when nobody complains, people working in a store have no way of knowing they are doing less than a perfect job.

Yes, the package that complaints come in is ugly, grotesque, and unpleasant, yet what is inside is of critical importance to you and your business — it is information about your business and about how customers perceive you that fifty other people didn't bother telling you. And what did those other fifty people do? You know exactly, because you've done it yourself: they simply left and never came back. So a "Thank you very much for taking the time to bring this to our attention" is legitimate, genuine, and necessary.

These Customers from Hell have also done something else that the other fifty people didn't bother doing: they've given you a second chance. They haven't "defected" or walked away forever just to tell all of their friends about their unpleasant experience. They've come to you and given you an opportunity to correct the situation. So you should also consider genuinely saying, "Thank you for giving us the opportunity to correct this situation."

Think about how your customers are likely to respond after you've said something like that. In all probability, they'll look at you with a certain amount of astonishment and simply say, "You're welcome." If they haven't said it already, they may even add, "Now what can we do about this?" Again, that's positive.

Whenever I take the time to fill out a store's comment or suggestion card, I'm always impressed when I receive a reply, particularly when the person makes a point of thanking me for taking the time to communicate with the company.

I spend around two hundred nights a year in hotels. I can tell you that over the years, I have stayed in some of the very best and some of the very scariest. Because of this, I tend to be very aware of the value and level of service I receive.

In Toronto, I once stayed at a very nice, posh, four-star hotel (which had the luxury of being able to charge five-star prices). When I arrived, I was quite distressed to find myself in a check-in line-up of five people, with only one person working at the front desk. This poor young man at the desk had to deal not only with the line-up but also with the telephones, which resulted in my waiting almost thirty minutes before getting my room.

The desk clerk was exceptionally pleasant and very apologetic for the delay. Nonetheless, the idea of paying $185 per night with such slow service didn't sit right with me. Rather than give the clerk a hard time — it wasn't his fault, after all

— I chose to fill out one of the hotel's comment cards with some fairly pointed remarks.

To my surprise and delight, five days later I received a telephone call from the hotel's general manager, who handled the situation beautifully. He listened intently to my complaint, probing and prompting until I had it all out of my system. He then said, "Mr. Belding, you had to wait thirty minutes in line?" I answered yes, to which he replied, "I certainly understand why that would upset you. It would upset me if I were in that position. It is quite distressing to me that your first impression of our hotel was one of inadequate service, and I want to thank you for bringing this to our attention. As you know, we are in a highly competitive business, and we can ill afford to have our customers perceive us in a poor light. If you hadn't informed us of your experience, we would never have realized there was a potential problem." Did I feel good about that hotel after our conversation? You bet I did.

Thanking somebody is an acknowledgement of the value of his input. It reinforces that you care about him and that he is important to your business. It is at this point in conflict that more often than not something magical happens: the confrontation simply disappears. Rather than looking into the eyes of an enraged, frustrated customer, you are now looking into the eyes of somebody who perceives you as a friend, an ally.

Let's pick up our toy-store example from the previous chapter and see how this next element moves the whole process along.

Dealing with the Customer from Hell

Customer: "I know it's not your fault — you don't make them — but it's really a nuisance bringing these things back. Particularly when I get scolded by some young clerk."

Salesperson: [*Echoing*] "You've been scolded for bringing something back?"

Customer: "Last week, a clerk suggested that I should have called the manufacturer instead of bringing it into the store. I don't want all that hassle. I thought you had a hassle-free return policy."

Salesperson: [*Thanking*] "We do, ma'am. Absolutely. Thank you very much for bringing this to our attention. The last thing we want is to make our customers uncomfortable."

Customer: "Well, of course you don't. And most of the people in here are quite nice . . ."

As you can see, the emotional states of the customer and the salesperson are now no longer part of the equation. The salesperson understands why the customer was frustrated, and the customer perceives the salesperson as an ally with whom she can talk. The stage is now set for a mutually beneficial solution to the problem.

. . . . .

Ten

Evaluating
Your Options

. . . .

Now is the time to think.
Now is the time to sort out the
options that are open to you.

. . . .

It may not seem as if you've been very proactive so far. You've simply taken the brunt of your customer's emotional state. If you've followed the steps that I've outlined to this point, you've listened to him, encouraged him to talk more, echoed some of the key issues in his mind, sympathized with the way he is feeling, and thanked him genuinely for his input. Put simply, you've successfully removed the negative emotional element from the equation.

It is hoped by this point that the two of you are on the

same team. You still have a problem to solve, but now you are able to do it together. This is the time to begin searching for what is commonly known as a win-win solution. Although it does require some effort on your part, a win-win solution is, more often than not, quite achievable.

THE WIN-WIN APPROACH

What do I mean by a win-win solution? A win-win solution allows both people to leave a conflict believing that the solution was fair for everybody. Win-win is an attitude, a state of mind; it is not just a series of techniques one can use to solve problems. As I suggested earlier, to resolve conflict you have to *want* to resolve conflict. A positive resolution is one that leaves everyone satisfied.

Non–win-win attitudes or states of mind are thoughts such as "How can I keep from getting screwed?" and "How can I get even with this customer?" Even thoughts such as "How can I appease this customer?" or "How can I make this customer happy?" will not lead to a win-win solution. The thought process must be "How can I resolve this to the benefit of both of us?"

Airlines, for example, use win-win solutions all the time. Let's say you go to check in for a flight. You've got a ticket, but the flight is overbooked. You're upset. Rather than simply turning you away, to have you defect to its competitor, the airline may bump you into a first-class seat. The benefit to you is a comfortable trip to your destination. The benefits to the airline are no additional cost (the seat was going to be empty anyway) and a satisfied customer who will keep coming back. If no first-class seats are available, an airline will often determine which customers are not in a great hurry and offer them a later flight in exchange for a complimentary ticket anywhere the airline flies. Those customers have the inconvenience of waiting, but they get the benefit down the road of a free flight. The airline, meanwhile, gains a happy customer and all it had to give up was a seat on a flight that likely wouldn't have been full anyway. Everyone wins.

One Saturday afternoon in one of my toy stores, a customer showed up to pick up a large play structure for her son. Owing to a series of mistakes (mostly by me), the structure wasn't ready. When the customer found out it wasn't there, she was furious. Her son's birthday was the next morning, and she had been promised it would be at the store on Saturday for her to pick up. She had already paid for it, and she wanted her money back to go to another store and get the product.

As I listened to her, I discovered that she lived forty miles out of town, and that she had made a considerable detour on her way back from work to buy the product at our store. She shopped in our store, she said, because she liked the service.

The play structure was half an hour away in our warehouse, and she didn't have time to wait while I went to pick it up and bring it back to the store. I listened, echoed her key issues, sympathized with her position, and thanked her for bringing the problem to my attention. I then asked what time the party was. She told me that it started at 11 a.m., and that it was being held at a local McDonald's. I told her I'd gladly give her money back if that's what she chose, but if she preferred, I would drive out to her house myself and, while the children were at the McDonald's, erect the play structure in her backyard so that it would be there as a surprise when they returned. She thought this solution was perfect.

The next day I delivered it and, just as an added touch, brought some gigantic red ribbon to wrap around the play structure. That was a win-win situation. The customer got what she wanted. And I kept the sale and a long-term, valuable customer at a cost of three hours of my time and five dollars in gas.

Think about what the other options were. What if I had just given her money back? That would have been a *lose-lose* situation. She would have been forced to go to another store, consuming at least another hour of her valuable time with no guarantee that the second store would have had the product either. I would have lost a sale, a valued, long-term customer, and all of her friends.

What if my store didn't have a cash return policy? What if I could offer only a credit note or an exchange? That could have led to a *win-lose* situation. I would have got to keep the money, but the customer would still not have had her play structure. The problem, of course, with a win-lose situation is that in the long run, the "winner" doesn't win at all. The customer would likely not have shopped in my store again, and she still would have told all of her friends about her unpleasant experience.

I also could have overreacted, giving away a bunch of free products. That would have been a *lose-win* situation. I would have been out an awful lot of money and she would have walked away with an awful lot of products that would very likely have made her child happy. Perhaps keeping the customer satisfied by overreacting might have paid off in the long run. But there was a better solution, I believe, and that's the one I chose.

TAKE TIME TO THINK

So how can you go about achieving a win-win solution? The first thing you need to do is buy some time. By that I mean a few seconds, no more. Drop a pen on the floor, rustle through some papers as though you're looking for something that might help. Do something, *anything,* that gives you a few moments to think.

Why do we do this? Remember that so far we've been focused only on gaining a better understanding of the problem and helping our customer gain control over his emotional state. If you've followed the steps as I've outlined them, you haven't yet begun to apply yourself to a solution to the problem. Now is the time to think. Now is the time to sort out the options that are open to you. Don't actually remove yourself physically from the situation — if you do that, all of the hard work you've put in may go for naught. But do try to give yourself a few moments to determine your options.

PROBE FOR OPTIONS

The evaluation stage is a time to probe for solutions that would be acceptable to your customer. Tell him what some of your options are and see if any of them strike a chord. Get him involved in the creative resolution process.

Start off with some very specific probing questions. You could ask, "Mr. Smith, you are a very valuable customer to us and it is very important to us that you are satisfied. Would a refund be acceptable to you?" If this is an appropriate and viable option, Mr. Smith will tell you so. If not, he will tell you that too, and he will usually tell you why it's not appropriate.

Let's take, for example, a woman who comes back into your store to return a dress that has torn at the seams. You know by looking at it that the dress is too small for her. In fact, you remember selling it to her, and she was insistent on buying things two sizes too small. But now she is back in your store complaining that you sell shoddy merchandise.

You listen intently to her complaint, echo the key issues, and then say, "Well, Mrs. Jones, from what you've told me, I sure can understand why you'd be frustrated. First of all, I'd like to thank you very much for bringing this to our attention and for giving us the opportunity to correct the situation. You're an important customer to us, and it's important to me that you are satisfied with everything in this store. Would a refund be acceptable to you?"

To this Mrs. Jones may reply, "I don't need a refund — I need a dress. I'm going out tomorrow night, and I don't have a dress to wear." You can then say, "Well, Mrs. Jones, we do have some other beautiful dresses (larger, but you don't have to say that), and I'm confident you won't have this problem again." Then Mrs. Jones may agree to look at the other dresses. Don't forget that it is your job, not the customer's, to search for options.

I purchased a new VCR on sale from a junior department

store one Christmas. We struggled to make it work for three weeks, and finally gave up when it ate a tape borrowed from a neighbour. I took the VCR back to the store.

I explained to a very pleasant woman in the customer-service department that an exchange would be great, but that the first VCR still had my neighbour's tape in it. She pointed me towards the electronics department and told me that the salesperson there should be able to look after both the exchange and extracting the tape.

I arrived at the electronics department and explained again what had happened. The salesperson asked a few questions while filling out some sort of return form, then looked up at me and said matter-of-factly, "Well, we've got lots of machines, but you're not gonna get your tape back."

"What?" I asked, a little startled.

"Sir," she said with a gentle scold and a you're-just-too-stupid-to-live expression, "we don't repair these *here*. They get sent *out* for repairs. I've got eight machines already on their way. I doubt very seriously that the repair shop is going to send back a tape."

Now, I hadn't walked in to the store prepared for a fight. I wasn't planning on being a Customer from Hell, but my back went up. "I need that tape," I stated very firmly. "It belongs to a neighbour and I have to return it." I was not giving up.

The woman looked at me as if I'd sprouted another nose. "Well, you're not likely to get it back from the repair place," she repeated. "Once it's out of here, it's out of my control."

"What if I open it up and take the tape out myself?" I asked.

Again the smirk and the head shake. "You'll void the warranty."

"Then give me the name of the repair place, and I will follow up to make sure I get back the tape," I persisted.

Again with the head. "If you want me to, I can give you the name of another place here in the city, and you can go and have your machine repaired yourself — still under warranty, of course. Then you'll probably get back the tape."

"This VCR is brand new. I don't want it repaired. I want a new one!" I wasn't raising my voice yet, but I was really starting to lose my patience.

"Then you won't get back your tape," she said. She just stood there looking at me.

I matched her gaze and her silence. After thirty seconds or so, she rolled her eyes and said, "I can call the manager if you like." I told her I thought that was a fine idea.

As we were waiting for the manager, the salesperson asked what tape it was. "It's one of the *Star Wars* tapes," I said. "I'm not sure which one."

"Well, we have the whole trilogy here," she said. "If you had just told me that, I could have given you one of those in the first place!"

Three minutes later, everything was settled. But not before I received one final scolding for not having a proper receipt.

Let's take a look at what happened here as it relates to LESTER so far. The salesperson listened to a certain degree as she was filling out the return form. She did not echo my key concerns, which caused me, later on in the discussion, to wonder if she in fact understood my predicament. She expressed no sympathy and certainly did not thank me.

She made no effort to evaluate what options were open to her until I persisted. What she did, in fact, was go straight to the response stage. And the response, of course, was "tough luck."

If we assume she had done everything else right, what could she then have done in the evaluation stage? What kind of probing questions could she have asked? Here are three, just for starters:

▶ "Is it a personal tape or a store-bought one?"
▶ "Would getting the machine repaired be acceptable to you, or do you definitely want a new one?"
▶ "Would a replacement tape be suitable?"

The argument perhaps could be made that since everything worked out in the end, what's the difference how I got there? I hope the answer to that is obvious. The difference is that I'm going to think twice before I go back there to shop. The difference is that the next time the customer may not be as well behaved as I was. The difference is that there *is* a better way. And look at the longer-term effects: I'm now writing about it in a book, and she probably went home that night to tell her husband about the Customer from Hell she met. Had she approached the situation with a win-win attitude, we both would likely have forgotten the transaction by the end of that day.

The most frequent mistake we make in managing difficult situations is that we tend to respond too quickly. We don't make a strong enough effort to thoroughly understand an issue, then explore all the options. Not only do we wind up contributing to the confrontation, but we very often find ourselves looking in the wrong places for solutions.

Think about the woman in the dress shop who had purchased an item too small for her. She was already embarrassed by having to return it, so why compound the problem by offering her an inappropriate solution?

KEEP CONTROL

Some people prefer the technique of just directly asking the customer to outline what it will take to fix the situation. "Sir, what will it take to make things right?" Asking a customer what it is he wants or what he feels will make the situation right has an interesting effect. First, a customer will usually ask far less of you than you would be prepared to give him. Also, with his emotional state now under control, he may actually be embarrassed to tell you what it is he really wants.

I suggest to you that this is not a terrific approach. If you use it, it should be as an absolute last resort. Look at it this way: if you leave it to the customer to tell you what he wants, you lose control of the situation and set yourself up for more potential conflict. If your customer becomes uncomfortable or embarrassed, then you have undone much of the good you accomplished in the first four stages.

IT'S NOT WHAT YOU SAY . . .

The way you use language is critical in the evaluation stage. Returning to the example of Mrs. Jones and the dress, notice that the salesperson said, "We do have some other beautiful dresses, and I'm confident you won't have this problem again." A less skilled salesperson might have said, "We do have some beautiful dresses, and I think if we get one a couple of sizes larger you won't encounter this problem again." The thought is the same, but in the second example the message is "Lady, you are fatter than you think you are."

Being conscious of how you say things also means avoiding the temptation to scold your customer for having made a mistake, or for not understanding your rules. This is particularly important when the customer's "mistake" is actually the result of a salesperson not doing her job properly in the first place.

Earlier in this chapter, I suggested that a good way to start the probing process might be to say, "Mr. Smith, you are a very valuable customer to us, and it is very important to us that you are satisfied . . ." It never hurts to be absolutely blatant in telling your customer how important he is (my daughter calls it sucking up).

I have a good friend, and now business partner, whom I believe would be a shoe-in for a Shameless Schmoozer of the Year Award. There is nothing he enjoys more than telling someone in no uncertain terms just how good he or she is. He lays it on thicker than paint on an old cottage. The thing is — everyone loves Bob. In all the years I have known him, I've never heard anyone say, "Geez, I hate that guy when he says all those wonderful things about me!" Bob is honest, open, and sincere with his praise. He also, not coincidentally, rarely finds himself involved in a confrontation.

The lesson from Bob, then, is don't be afraid to lay it on a little thick in telling customers how important they are. They won't object, I promise.

DON'T MAKE YOUR CUSTOMERS FEEL STUPID

Often, when a salesperson has not accurately enough determined a customer's needs, the customer will come back complaining that the product is defective or unsuitable. Many customers will select an inappropriate product because it was less expensive, but they do not fully recognize that it will not suit their needs. They may buy too small a photocopier, or shoes that are the wrong colour, or a two-door car when they really need a four-door car.

Is this the "stupid customer's own fault" for buying something that was wrong for him? No, it reflects a failure on the part of the original salesperson. And if the salesperson had outlined the risks of purchasing an inappropriate product in the first place, chances are the customer would not have come back angry, upset, frustrated, or unsatisfied.

I remember, for example, when I bought my first computer for business. Back then, I had a choice between an XT, a 286, and a 386. The XTs were the slowest on the market and were quickly becoming outdated. The 386 had just been introduced and was considerably more expensive than the 286. The salesperson listened to what I would be using the computer for and recommended the 386. "The 286 will do the job," she said, "but it likely won't be too long before most software will require the capabilities of a 386 simply to run. If you buy a 286, chances are you will be coming back here within two years to upgrade. You may find it less expensive and more productive in the long run if you simply go with a 386 now."

I figured this was simply part of the salesperson's spiel, took a chance, and bought the 286. Sure enough, eighteen months later, any new software I wanted to buy simply wouldn't run on my machine. I ended up having to buy a new one.

Oh, I was frustrated all right. And I was angry. But I was angry at myself for not having listened in the first place. When I went back to get my new computer, the salesperson resisted the temptation to make me feel even more stupid by saying something subtle, such as "I told you so!" I appreciated that. I picked out my new computer, and she recommended that I increase the amount of memory capacity. This time I listened, and I was glad I did.

We must be very certain, and should have very compelling reasons, before we start chastising our customers for making poor purchase decisions. For one thing, most purchase decisions should have been influenced by a salesperson. And even when a customer knowingly makes a poor decision, it does no good to scold him for it. "Well, madam," the salesperson in the dress shop might have said, "I told you not to buy something that small." It doesn't do you any good to embarrass your customer.

KEEP THE END IN SIGHT

It is important during the evaluation process that you not let your emotions get in the way. You may, for instance, feel that a customer is lying to you, or that she is just trying to pull the wool over your eyes or take advantage of you. Even if you feel this way, you must think very carefully about the impact of your actions. Think about the value of that customer. If she walks away unsatisfied — even if she was lying to you — how many people is she going to tell? Where are they going to shop after she tells them? How much business, in the long run, will this cost you?

Eleven

Responding to
the Situation

*The secret is not to let the guidelines,
the rules, or the lines of authority stand in the
way of resolving the situation. Sometimes this
means you have to get creative.*

Once you have evaluated the situation and determined
the options that are open to you and the options that are
suitable to your customer, you must respond. Now is the time
to solve the problem. Now is the time to act.

As I've discussed, perhaps the single most common mistake salespeople in difficult situations make is to jump
straight to this stage, ignoring the five previous steps. Interestingly, there is another type of salesperson who rarely, if
ever, reaches this stage. This is the Order-Taker, who takes

down all the information, promises to pass the complaint along, but never actually does anything about it. Then there are the Dismissers, those who evaluate the situation and determine what the response should be, but don't bother following through because it's just going to be too much hassle.

A wonderful illustration of the importance of responding effectively, instead of being non-responsive, came to me when I was having a problem with my laptop computer. The whole story unfolded over a six-week period. I was in a large city, many hundreds of miles from my home, meeting with some of our existing clients and preparing for a huge presentation to a prospective new client. My two-year-old laptop chose that particular moment to die on me, with this very important presentation locked inside it.

Needless to say, I was a trifle worried. I dug up the 1-800 number of the manufacturer's twenty-four-hour service line, negotiated my way through the intricate voicemail system, and finally managed to get a living, breathing human being. The young man (at least, he sounded young) was fabulous. He started off by doing a nifty little over-the-phone diagnosis of the computer, and determined that the problem was a "CMOS register test failure." He then explained to me that this was usually an indicator that the computer's motherboard was shot, and that the motherboard was the heart and soul of the computer. "There is a slim chance," he added, "that it's just that the CMOS battery is dead, in which case it's not a serious problem at all." He continued to advise me on the procedure for having the computer repaired, which began with "First you package the computer in a box and send it to . . ."

Responding to the Situation

When I explained my situation to him and informed him that I needed a solution within the next thirty hours, there was a pause on the end of the line. With a tremendous amount of empathy in his voice, he said, "Mr. Belding, our company doesn't have a procedure or a system in place for solving problems that quickly, and there's really not much I can do at the moment. I sure understand your situation, though. What I can do, perhaps, is give you some other options for having it fixed." He then listed off four or five things I could try, but made it clear that he wasn't sure any of them would work. "Good luck!" he said at the end.

When I hung up, I was feeling pretty good. The representative had listened very carefully, quickly identified that my biggest problem at the moment was a time problem, and let me know that he sympathized with my situation. He then demonstrated that he cared by providing a number of possible solutions that fell well outside company policy. Wow! I thought. This company really gets it! Unfortunately, that thought lasted for only a few minutes.

I began to follow up on the representative's suggestions. One of the next calls I made ended up with me being re-routed all the way back to the same call centre this first representative worked in. I won't go into the details of what ensued, but suffice it to say that I had perhaps the worst customer-service experience of my life. I was scolded for attempting to find alternative channels to having my computer fixed. I was told that the first representative was incompetent and should never have given me the options he did. I was told that there was no possible way to have my computer fixed in a thirty-hour period, and that if I tried to have someone outside the company fix it, I might be in Serious Trouble.

Over and over again, I explained that this was important to me, that money was no object, and that I was simply looking for whatever suggestions anyone could offer. Over and over again, the second representative made it clear that I was a huge pain in the butt. Finally, in exasperation, I said, "I don't think you understand. I'm five hundred miles from home, I have a critical presentation to give in a day and a half, and I've got a damn computer that won't work!" He hung up on me.

This was a Dismisser, someone who had no interest in making my problem his. The worst part of the story, however, is still to come. I decided to get hold of a supervisor to let someone know how I had been treated. After leaving six messages for various supervisors and managers, all of which went unanswered, I wrote a letter to the international executive vice-president. At this point, I was no longer upset (I had had the computer fixed at a local dealer for thirty dollars), but I did think that he might appreciate knowing about this chink in his company's armour.

Six weeks later, I got a call from a local manager to whom my letter had finally drifted. He listened to my story, and I told him of the unanswered telephone calls. He thanked me very much for my input, told me that customer service was very important to the company, and said that he would be making a report about this for his boss. That was it. He took the order.

Although he had followed most of the steps of LESTER and was very pleasant, I still felt a little . . . well, unsatisfied.

Something was missing. He didn't give me a sense of closure, of completeness. After all of the time that had gone by, it wasn't enough.

RESPOND INSTANTLY

The first and most important rule of responding is to respond instantly. Statistics show that more than 75 percent of complaining customers will remain your customers if you solve the problem. But more than 90 percent will remain your customers if you solve the problem instantly.

This often poses a problem for people in retail, because many companies do not give their employees a great deal of discretion. It may very well be that what the customer wants is something that can be approved only by the manager or by head office. In some retail chains, even the managers do not have a lot of options for satisfying their customers. But the last thing you want to do is hand the problem off. Even if you are in this situation you can still respond instantly. You may not be able to *solve* the problem instantly, but you can *respond* instantly. What you need to communicate to your customer is that you do not have the authority to resolve the situation, but that you are going to take it upon yourself to make sure that the situation gets resolved.

If you are in a position of not being the ultimate decision-maker, I suggest you try something like this: "Mr. Smith, this is something my manager usually looks after, but it is very important to me that you are satisfied. If it is okay with you, I would like to get your name, telephone number, and address so that I can personally see to it that this gets resolved." This reinforces to the customer that you do truly care, and that you are on his side. It also saves him from having to rejustify his position to yet another person.

In a difficult situation, customers are looking for a sign that you care. Most rational people will understand when something is beyond your control or your authority. Most people understand that you have to operate within guidelines established by your company, just as they do with the companies they work for. The secret is to not let the guidelines, the rules, or the lines of authority stand in the way of resolving the situation. Sometimes this means you have to be creative.

A wonderful story was related to me by the manager of a large shopping centre who had purchased a rug shampooer from a major, well-known department store. He wrestled the large and bulky box that the shampooer came in to the front cash, paid for it, and took it home. One week later, the same shampooer in the same store went on sale for 20 percent less! He went to the store with his receipt to see if they would credit him the difference. The woman at the "customer service" desk informed him in no uncertain terms that store policy clearly stated that sale prices applied only to merchandise purchased during the sale period. Although she didn't say it in exactly these words, the message was "Tough luck."

My friend then asked if he could return the product and get his money back. Absolutely, she said. The store had a no-hassle, money-back guarantee. My friend, getting somewhat agitated, then said, "Okay, so you are telling me that I have to bring the product back, get my money refunded, and then go and pick out a new one and purchase it at the sale price?" She looked at him like he was some kind of con artist but said, "Well, I suppose you could do that."

So my friend drove back to the house, picked up the shampooer, drove it back to the store, went to the "customer service" desk (interesting name for it, given the circumstances), and got a cash refund for the product. He then carried the product back around to the checkout and repurchased it at the sale price.

Technically, the woman at the customer-service desk did nothing wrong. She was following the rules and regulations set by her company — rules and regulations over which she had no control. The creative solution to the problem, however, would have been for her simply to give him the cash difference, then ring through both the return and the new sale on her terminal after he was gone. The net outcome would have been the same for the store but much, much more positive for the consumer. The best solutions, win-win solutions, are almost always creative solutions.

Think of union negotiations. One side takes posture A, the other side takes posture B. The ultimate solution is almost never A or B, nor is it a compromise — something between A or B. The win-win solution is usually something entirely different: C, D, E, or F.

WHEN APPROPRIATE, FESS UP

If, after you've listened to your customer, it turns out that you have actually done something wrong, don't be afraid to swallow your pride and accept responsibility. Tell your customer you goofed. Let him know it was entirely your fault (if it was). Don't make excuses or give the customer good reasons as to why it happened. Simply accept responsibility.

If a mistake was made by someone else in your store, then accept responsibility on behalf of the store, but don't point your finger at the other salesperson. In other words, don't say, "Yes, you are right. Sheila really messed up this time." Now is the time for the royal "we." "Yes, you are right. We sure messed up this time." If the customer perceives you to be passing off blame to someone else, you will lose credibility instantly.

FOLLOWING UP

The final principle of responding is perhaps the most important because this is your opportunity to turn what was a negative situation into a positive one. It is your chance to turn a potentially "defecting" customer into a long-term, loyal patron of your store. This final principle is to follow up. Following up is especially important if you had to pass off a decision to the manager.

Consider this situation. A customer is irate because there isn't suitable wheelchair access to your store. There is nothing that you, the employee, can do about it, but you say that you will certainly bring it to the attention of your manager. You do, and the manager responds by widening the aisles in the store and informing the customer of the action that has been taken.

What if, one week later, you phone the customer and say, "Hello, Mr. Jones, it's Shaun Belding calling from XYZ store at the Waterfront Mall. I was the one you spoke to about the wheelchair-accessibility problem. I was just calling to see if the problem has been resolved to your satisfaction."

How do you think your customer would respond to this? Wow! he'll probably think. You really do care! Do you suppose he'll tell his friends about his experience? You bet he will, but now it will be in a positive light instead of a negative one.

By following up on a difficult situation once it has been resolved, you solidify your relationship with your customer and, at the same time, make yourself an ambassador for your store. Such ambassadors cannot be replaced by all the advertising in the world.

3

All Hell Breaks Loose

*Consider your origin; you were not born
to live like brutes* — DANTE'S INFERNO

Twelve

The Unreasonable Customer

· ·

The number of customers
who are truly unreasonable
is very small indeed.

· ·

L et's try to put this into perspective. In the world of
Customers from Hell, many of the situations are taken
care of quite effectively by using the principles of LESTER.
Many will also simply disappear as we become better salespeople — as defined in chapter 3 of this book. This leaves us
with a handful whom we call unreasonable customers.

If we agree that Customers from Hell are a tiny minority
of the total number of customers that we see each year, then
the number of those who are truly unreasonable is very small

indeed. We do encounter them from time to time, however, and this chapter is dedicated to techniques for dealing with these very specific situations.

This chapter is a laundry list of the various kinds of unreasonable customers. They are listed in no particular order. Unlike LESTER, which applies globally to unsatisfied customers, the solution to each type of unreasonable customer behaviour is unique. As near as I have been able to determine, there is no single surefire method for handling all the different types of unreasonable customers.

THE TIME VAMPIRE

I remember Sandy, a new employee with about three months' worth of experience under her belt. She had just come in for her usual 6 p.m. shift and was telling me about her experience of the night before. It seemed that a customer had kept her a full hour past closing time. "Are you nuts?" I said to her. "Why didn't you just tell her to leave?" "I tried," said Sandy, "but I just couldn't get her to go." I harrumphed a bit at that, muttered something about being more assertive, and wandered off shaking my head.

Two days later, I met the same customer and the same thing happened to me. I remember dropping subtle hints — "Oh, looks like the mall's closed . . . I guess I'd better lock up the store" — and then trying subtler hints like turning off most of the lights in the store and counting the cash. All this woman did was talk and talk and talk. In the hour and a half that she was there, I learned all about her children, her husband, many of the medical ailments she had, and every good deed she had done since she was six years old. It didn't seem to matter what I said or did, nothing dissuaded her.

This woman is a time vampire. We meet them in all shapes and sizes. Sometimes they are friends who come in to visit with us when we're trying to work. Sometimes they are customers who want to socialize with us when we have a busy store. Time vampires are both a tremendous source of frustration and a very real liability to a business.

After my little episode, I took it upon myself to learn how to deal with this particular type of Customer from Hell. It took a lot of painful trial and error, but I finally came up with a solution that works pretty much all of the time. The first thing is to understand what makes these people time vampires. What's motivating them? Well, chances are they're lonely and have a desperate need to be heard. They have a tremendous lack of social skills and no understanding of some of the basic social graces. But the most important thing to be aware of is that they do not recognize that their actions are inappropriate. They confuse politeness on the part of the other person with a desire to listen to them. They perceive hints such as "Gee, it's almost closing time" as a desire on your part to share information. Like most social faux pas, the behaviour is neither deliberate nor malicious.

Time vampires are almost always self-focused. They are completely unaware of your needs and your perception of the situation. They also have you at a disadvantage, because they're playing by a set of social rules (their own) that are completely different from the ones with which you are familiar.

The solution to handling a time vampire is, intellectually, very easy. It does, however, require breaking some of the social rules you grew up with, which can be quite an emotional challenge. The solution may also at first appear very harsh to you. It will very likely go against your most basic sense of what is right and what is wrong, what is socially acceptable and what is not. The key, though, is to remember that these people are not getting the subtle clues. Subtlety doesn't work with time vampires.

What does work is being brutally direct, even abrupt — almost to the point of being rude. Believe it or not, a "gentle clue" to a time vampire is the equivalent of a two-by-four over the head for most people. It's a three-step process:

- *Gentle Clue #1* is to put a physical barrier between the two of you. You accomplish this with body language. Put both of your hands in front of you, as if to push the person away. Look into her eyes. Let her know in no uncertain terms that it is your turn to talk.
- *Gentle Clue #2* is to then say something very direct and frank, such as "I'd love to keep talking with you, but I am afraid that you will have to leave."
- *Gentle Clue #3* is to instantly turn your back to the time vampire (before she has a chance to wind herself back up again) and walk away. If it's closing time, walk to the door and wait for her to come out with you.

Simple, huh? Right. If somebody did this to you, you would surely find this as offensive as I would. But trust me on this one, time vampires will not find it offensive in the least. In fact, the beauty of this technique is that each time they come back (and they will come back), the clues you have to leave them become subtler and subtler. While they may never actually understand why you can't spend all that time with them, they will begin to recognize the pattern.

I don't want to leave you with the impression that time vampires are all thick and stupid. They're not. Many time vampires I've met are highly intellectual people who are either insecure or just socially unskilled. I expect they would be devastated if they knew how much of a challenge they are to people, and how much negative impact they have on a business.

THE PERMISSIVE PARENT

The first universal truth about parents is that they all consider the things their kids do "cute." Another universal truth about parents is that no two have the same set of standards or expectations for their children.

If you've been in retail for more than a month, chances are you have met a parent who seemingly has no control over his or her child. The child runs rampant through the store, destroying displays, pulling merchandise off shelves, and being a general annoyance to your other customers. I list this as an unreasonable customer (the parent, not the child), because the parent unreasonably expects that you and your other customers should accept that kind of behaviour from his or her child.

It's a tough situation to deal with. On the one hand, you don't want someone's child disrupting the store or damaging merchandise. But on the other hand, you don't want to offend a parent who is, presumably, a customer. Nevertheless, you have to do something. The cost of not acting can be too great. It is not just that there is great potential for the child to do some serious damage, either to himself or to the store, but that there is also the very real negative impact an untamed child can have on other customers.

If the other customers in the store get irritated, they will not have a pleasant shopping experience. If they do not have a pleasant shopping experience, they are far less likely to make a purchase and will remember that unpleasant experience the next time they consider shopping in your store. If you don't at least attempt to resolve the situation, you run the risk of having your customers leave your store thinking, "Why didn't they do something about that child?" or "How could they let that child run wild like that?" In the minds of the customers, "they" includes you.

I think we all recognize that the child is most often not really the problem. Children at a young age generally act within the parameters set by their parents. In the child's mind, what he is doing is acceptable because his parents have never told him that it isn't. It's also likely that the parent is taking no action because she believes that everyone else finds her child and her child's actions as "cute" as she does (our first universal truth).

It is, of course, always possible that it's not the child at all. You must consider the possibility that it just might be your own low tolerance level for children. In all fairness, some people get distressed by everything children do. If you have a low tolerance level for children and the way they behave generally, don't make the assumption that other people feel the same way. Before you take action, be sure that the child is actually disturbing other people or doing something that is destructive to the store. It is important that you make the distinction between a boisterous, happy child and a child who is creating mischief. If, however, the child is creating a disturbance that is affecting the other customers, they will most certainly appreciate your taking action. Their frustration will increase if you do not take action.

There are two effective ways of dealing with an untamed child. They seem to work equally well depending on your own personality. The first one is to make a joke out of it. I had a young man working for me who was very adept at this lighthearted technique. Kent would bound up to a child who was busily tearing merchandise off the shelf, squat down in front of him, and with a great big smile and a voice loud enough for the parent and the other customers to hear, say, "Why are you tearing my store apart?" The child would usually answer with only a big grin, but inevitably the parents would recognize that their child had been doing something inappropriate and pull in the reins.

Obviously, this lighthearted approach is not one that everyone would be comfortable using. Nor is it a technique that everyone could execute credibly. The successful use of this approach requires a very outgoing, confident personality. If you're comfortable with being lighthearted, then try it. If you're not comfortable with this approach, don't.

The second method, for those of us who prefer a more conservative approach, is to confront the parent directly and express concern for the safety of the child. You may want to say, "Oh, excuse me, ma'am, but I'm just a little concerned about your child. He may pull one of those racks over on top of himself, and I'd hate to see him get hurt." Whether the parents see through this particular facade is unimportant. What is important is that it works, and that it allows the parents to save face in front of the other customers and in front of you.

THE SEXUAL HARASSER

Sexual harassment from a customer, which fortunately is very rare, is an extreme type of negative behaviour. One could quite easily fill the pages of this book with nothing but strategies to manage sexual harassment. And in fact, many excellent books have been written on the subject. If you are experiencing any form of sexual harassment, I recommend you seek out appropriate resource people for advice. It is not something to take lightly.

If I can pass along one important rule of thumb, however, it is this: if you are being sexually harassed by a customer, remove yourself from the situation instantly. Don't apologize, don't explain, don't excuse yourself. Simply walk away and go directly to somebody in authority, such as a manager. If you are alone in your store, then leave the store and seek out somebody in security. Don't worry about people stealing things from the store because you've left. There is no inventory in the world that is worth more than your emotional and physical well-being. I will even go so far as to say that if your manager does not agree with this philosophy, seek employment elsewhere with someone who cares about you. If you are a manager, your role in supporting your employees is critical. If someone comes to you complaining about being sexually harassed by a customer, do not take it lightly. Act immediately.

Having said all this, I recognize that dealing with sexual harassment is one of those concepts that is easy to put on paper but not so easy to put into practice. Walking away from a customer goes against everything we've ever been taught. Not only will you feel that you're being rude, but you will also be losing a customer and all of his friends. It's not easy to do. All I can tell you is that walking away beats the alternatives.

As a retail manager, I had to deal with the sexual harassment of one of my staff, and the experience left a lasting impression on me. There was a man who frequented one of our stores and whom we knew only as "Paul's father." He was an abrasive man with a booming voice and an untamed four-year-old child. We always had advance notice that Paul's father was coming into our store because Paul (not his real name) usually preceded him by about five minutes.

Every time the routine was the same. Paul would run into the store and head straight for the play area. Five minutes later, Paul's father would walk into the store, stand four feet inside the front door, and in his loud voice bellow, "Paul? Paul? Where are you, Paul?" All the while, he was looking around, making sure that people were noticing him. He very rarely, if ever, purchased anything, but he consumed much of our staff's time by asking a lot of Very Important–Sounding Questions. I thought of him simply as a nuisance and a boor, and thus paid very little attention to him.

One evening, at a restaurant where I was hosting an informal employee recognition dinner, the subject of Paul's father came up in casual conversation. Apparently he had been making some rather bold remarks to one of my young employees. She considered him a harmless, if obnoxious, idiot and spent fifteen minutes telling us stories. She thought it was a big joke and had us all in hysterics as she told us about some of the stupid things he did. "He was in this afternoon," she said with a chuckle. "He just walked straight up to me, stared at my breasts, said, 'Ooh-la-la,' and then walked away. This guy's got to get a life!" When I asked her if Paul's father was bothering her, she just laughed and said, "No, I've seen a lot worse." So I put Paul's father out of my mind.

About a month later, the young woman who had been the object of Paul's father's affection left to go to college full time, at which time Paul's father shifted his attention to another young employee. Unfortunately, she didn't find him nearly as amusing. "What an idiot!" she said to me at one point in exasperation. "Can I tell him to take a hike?"

Right then, I made a classic managerial mistake. Because the first employee had dismissed Paul's father as a harmless moron and considered his behaviour a joke, so did I. As a result, I did not take the second employee's complaint seriously. That is, until a week later, when she phoned me at home in tears, asking me again for permission to tell him off. It was then that I realized how profoundly Paul's father was affecting her, and how helpless she must have felt when I failed to respond the first couple of times she brought it up. I promised her that I would deal with the situation the very next time he came into the store.

I was now faced with a dilemma. First, he had never made any of these comments in my presence. Second, his comments had been restricted to innuendo and subtle suggestions. In confronting him, there were no specific statements I could use to support my position. If I was challenged on the specifics, I would have no choice but to reply that he had told one of my employees that her sweatshirt really looked nice on her. Third, given Paul's father's loud and obnoxious manner, I knew it could very easily escalate into an unpleasant scene. Nevertheless, I refused to allow anybody to abuse one of my employees.

So I planned my strategy, and when he came through the door two days later I took a deep breath and confronted him. I asked if I could speak with him for a moment, then ushered him discreetly out the front door of the store to a quiet corner in the hall. I was very direct and very blunt with him. "I've had some complaints from my employees about some of the things you are saying to them," I began. "And these comments are making my employees extremely uncomfortable. I'm afraid I have to ask you not to shop in my store any more."

I steeled myself for a loud and accusatory "What the hell are you talking about?" but it never came. Instead, he took a small step back. His eyes started darting to and fro. He backed away, talking under his breath like a scolded child. "Oh, I didn't know," he mumbled. "I had no idea." And with that, he turned and walked away. We never saw him again.

I have since had several other similar encounters. And as a manager, I have learned one very valuable lesson about sexual harassment: when confronted by an authority figure, the sexual harasser will usually back down. When not confronted by an authority figure, the sexual harasser will continue his or her behaviour. This means that if you are being harassed, you need to get someone in authority involved. And if you are a manager, you must respond to your employees' needs immediately.

One final note about sexual harassment. It is common for people who have been harassed to second-guess themselves and wonder if maybe they were just being overly sensitive. While this may very well be true in some cases, I suggest that it is not generally true of people who work in retail. People who work in retail deal with tens of thousands of customers every year. We very quickly develop rather thick skins. Overly sensitive people do not survive in a retail environment.

THE BULLY

As is the case with sexual harassers, people who physically threaten salespeople are an extreme type of Customer from Hell. Fortunately, these customers are also quite rare. They should, however, be handled very carefully. People who physically threaten or use physically threatening body language are emotionally troubled and can be quite unpredictable.

If you ever find yourself feeling physically threatened, there is but one objective and that is to protect yourself. The best strategy, as with sexual harassment, is to remove yourself instantly from the situation. Again, don't apologize, don't excuse yourself, don't explain yourself — just very quickly remove yourself from the customer's presence and find someone in authority. If you are by yourself, find somebody in security or dial 911 and call the police. This is not the time to be concerned about looking foolish or as if you are overreacting. I have heard many stories of physically abusive customers that have sent chills up and down my spine.

A grocery store cashier I met in a training session told me of a situation that had happened the day before, when a customer literally tried to jump across the counter because he thought she had rung something in wrong. A salesperson in a high-end women's clothing store once described to me how she was pinned against a wall by an irate husband who wanted a cash refund.

Whatever you do, don't take this as an opportunity to scold the customer about his behaviour. If you have a physically abusive customer in an agitated state and you turn and say to him, "Sir, I find your behaviour quite inappropriate," you are only asking for trouble. As a rule, these people are not used to dealing with situations intellectually. Just get away.

GARBAGE MOUTH

At one time or another, most of us in retail have encountered a customer who has chosen to use foul language when dealing with us. Although I am presenting this person as an unreasonable kind of customer, I think you will discover that LESTER will usually help you deal with the situation. I bring up the swearing customer separately because sometimes we respond to these people in a fashion that can be very counterproductive and only intensify confrontation.

Customers swear in difficult situations for really only one

reason: they are frustrated, and it is the only way they know how to express themselves. For many, it is simply a normal way of speaking. Let's face it, we've all met people who can't seem to put a single sentence together without using a four-letter word. Confronting them with it by saying, "Sir, please don't swear" will only make matters worse. If swearing happens to be part of a person's normal way of speaking, then he will perceive it as a personal criticism. If he is swearing because he is fed up to the teeth, scolding him isn't going to make life any easier for either of you.

When somebody swears during a difficult situation, just ignore it. Listen intently to what the problem is, echo the key issues (without the swear words, of course), sympathize with the situation, and thank the customer for his input. You will find that if you have adequately controlled your own emotional state and have followed the first four steps of LESTER, the customer will very often correct his own behaviour. Remember that once you have removed the confrontation aspect of conflict and stepped to their side, the customer's emotional state will begin to settle down. Very often, if you've handled the situation properly, the customer will turn to you and say, "I'm sorry for the way I was talking. I'm just so frustrated."

Most swearing customers know that what they are doing is wrong, and they know that it is inappropriate. But they don't know how to react any better. In those very rare situations when the swearing is intense or is directed at you personally, it becomes more difficult to ignore. When this happens, you should, rather than scolding them, try to put the customer's behaviour into the context of the issue at hand. Let him understand in a gentle way that you want to address the problem, but that his behaviour is making it difficult for you to function.

So instead of saying, "Please don't swear," try saying, "Sir, I really want to resolve this as best I can, but when you speak to me like that, I just can't think straight." This places the emphasis on your emotional state rather than on the customer's behaviour. It doesn't work in all cases, but it minimizes the risk of magnifying the conflict.

HELL'S ACCOUNTANT

There are some customers out there who just love to tell you how much more expensive your products are than those of your competition. We had one customer who used to come in once a week. She was a good customer and spent thousands of dollars with us. But every time she came into the store, she made a point of telling us how much cheaper some of our products were at our competition. I can tell you that she drove us nuts. I used to make excuses and explain our prices by saying, "Well, yes, they probably do have products that are less expensive than ours, just as we have products that are often less expensive than theirs."

It took me a while, but I finally realized that she wasn't doing this to upset me or belittle the store, but that as a loyal customer, she felt it was her responsibility to advise me about what the competition was doing. I soon learned to simply say, "Oh, really? Thank you very much for letting me know." She would smile and say, "Well, I know it's important to you to know what other people are doing."

Of course, not all customers are telling you about a competitor's lower prices out of loyalty. They often follow their statement by asking if you will match the other store's price. If your store does not price match and this happens, there are a couple of different strategies you can take. The easiest is to smile nicely and say, "Oh, I would love to, but I don't have the authority to do that. I can get the manager, however. You are welcome to speak with her."

What this does, first of all, is let the customer know that you are on her side and that you are willing to do your part to satisfy her by getting the person who has the authority to make those kinds of decisions. About half of the customers you try this with will respond, "Oh no, never mind," and make the purchase anyway. They do this because they're as uncomfortable with confrontation and negotiation as you are. The downside to this strategy is that you are, in effect, saying, "It's not my table," and passing the customer off to someone else. As I've discussed, this can make people uncomfortable.

A better strategy is to deal with the situation proactively. You don't want to apologize for your prices (they pay your wages, after all), but you also want to make sure that you don't make your customer feel cheap for having tried to negotiate with you. Simply thank him for his input, let him know you are on his side, and reassure him that your prices are fair. Try something like this: "My, that is an excellent price, sir, and I appreciate your letting us know. I'd love to help, but our store has a long-standing policy of not matching prices because we feel it may not be fair to the customers who have paid full price. Our prices are competitive, however, and we'll be around should you ever have a problem."

This approach thanks the customer for his input, reiterates the policy while gently explaining the rationale for it, and then reassures the customer that he is getting good value. If you have the courage, it is always best to end your statement by trying to close the sale. You could, for example, say, "Can I take that to the cash for you?" or "Would you like to look at some accessories to go with that?" You will be amazed at how many customers will simply drop the issue and make the purchase.

Customers often raise the issue of price, but research shows that price is a primary motivation in less than one out of four purchase decisions. If your customer service has been superior to that of the other store, three out of four people will pay the higher price and purchase the item from you. When they ask about price, they are usually just saying, "Reassure me that I'm getting good value."

MISTAKEN MARY

At some point, a customer is going to walk into your store with a product you know you've never seen before and ask to return it. The conflict usually starts when the salesperson looks at the product and says, "No, ma'am, you didn't buy this here," making the customer feel a little stupid.

Some people are not comfortable with the possibility of being wrong, and they will react by asserting that it must be you, the clerk, who's mistaken. The key to preventing confrontation is in the very first words you say. So rather than saying, "No, we don't sell that," start by saying, "Oh, goodness, I haven't seen this before. Do you remember how long ago it was that you purchased it?" Or "Do you by any chance have your receipt?" After the customer has answered (they never have a receipt, of course), double-check to make sure you are correct that the store has not sold that product before. The next step is to return to the customer with a problem-solving answer instead of just a flat-out no.

For example, you might try saying, "I wonder if you could have purchased this at our competitor's, across the street. We often get confused with them." Don't risk embarrassing your customer. Give him an opportunity to bow out gracefully. If, however, he remains adamant, make sure that he understands you are not arguing with him. Make a point of checking with your co-workers and the files. Say to the customer, "Well, you may very well be right. Let me just double-check again." Do everything in your power to let the customer know you are on his side.

Sometimes the customer is looking to return something that your store does carry, but that he purchased at a competitor's store. He could be doing it because it costs more in your store and he figures he can make a couple of bucks on it by returning it this way. More likely, though, it's probably just more convenient for him to return it to your store.

Unless your company has a strict policy of not accepting returns without a receipt, I recommend you take the product back with a big smile and don't make an issue of it. Yes, you might lose a couple of bucks in the transaction, but you stand to make it back a hundredfold over the years with a satisfied customer.

WISHY-WASHY WENDY

There are some people in this world who simply can't make up their own minds. They'll hem and haw and drone on, saying, "Well, I'm just not sure." When you hear this, one of two things has happened — either they need reassurance or you haven't closed the sale.

1. *They need reassurance.*
Indecisive customers are often looking for reassurance about their purchase. The tricky part is trying to determine precisely what it is they need reassurance about. Sometimes they are so vague that trying to divine the roadblock is like trying to put toothpaste back into the tube.

Start off by restating your understanding of the customer's needs, and outlining why you believe your recommendation is appropriate. For example, say, "You had indicated that you were hoping to find a CD player for your daughter. You wanted something portable and durable, but you didn't want to spend a lot of money. From what you've told me, I think this particular model would suit your needs perfectly."

The next step is a very direct question, such as "Is there something I've missed? What is it you're unsure of?" Now comes the tricky part. The very nature of indecisive customers is that they are not comfortable telling you what it is they are unsure about. Once you have asked the questions, you must be very patient, listen very, very carefully, and read between the lines. You may have to ask some very specific, probing questions, such as "Are you comfortable with the brand? Are you comfortable that this will do the job for you? Is it within your budget?"

At some point, the indecisive customer will likely say, "Oh, it's just a little thing really . . ." or "Oh, I know it's no big deal, but . . ." and that's your clue. When an indecisive customer tells you it's no big thing, you know it is huge in her mind.

You see, indecisive customers are often so concerned with making a mistake that it paralyzes them. They continually run "what if?" scenarios through their minds. What if I get home and find I paid too much for it? What if I get home and my husband gives me grief for it? What if it becomes obsolete in three months? What if, what if, what if?

The first thing to be aware of is that if you in any way trivialize their concerns, you will lose them instantly. Let them know that you understand what they are feeling. Throw a couple of "what ifs" out there yourself and give them a worst-case scenario. Let's say, for example, that a customer says, "Well, it's not a big thing, really. I'm just not sure that I haven't seen this sweater for a better price." A salesperson can respond, "Oh, I know the feeling. What if you find out you could have got it a little bit cheaper somewhere else? That bothers me every time I go shopping. Or even worse, what if you buy it here and find it for 50 percent off somewhere else?"

The salesperson has now created what is commonly known as a straw man — a scenario that is designed to be easily knocked down. The salesperson might accomplish this by saying, "Well, thankfully, in our store we have a complete money-back guarantee, so if that happens you can bring it back in an instant." Or, if it's true, you can say, "Well, I don't think you'll find a significant difference in price from store to store here" (with emphasis on the word "significant"). Give it a moment to sink in, see if your indecisive customer is solemnly nodding her head, then proceed instantly with a solid assumed close: "Now, would you like to look at the accessories that go with that?" Whatever you do, don't give the customer the opportunity to think up another "what if?" Close the sale.

A common element of many sales training programs is "overcoming objections." I feel quite strongly that "objections" is a misleading term. Customers don't object to a product or to services, but they do have concerns about making poor purchase decisions. For indecisive customers these concerns are very, very real, and it is important that you don't try to gloss over them.

2. *You didn't close the sale.*

Customers who don't make decisions easily don't necessarily have indecisive personalities. More likely, they simply appear indecisive because the salesperson did not close the sale. I have observed this scene literally hundreds of times: a salesperson conducts a perfect sales interview, right up to presenting the perfect product, then stands there with the product in her hand, waiting for the customer to say, "Okay, I'll take it." Because the salesperson is no longer in control of the situation, the customer wavers for a brief moment, then says, "Well, I'm going to think about it for a while . . ." The customer walks away, and the salesperson says, "I guess she wasn't ready to buy yet."

The easiest way of preventing indecisive behaviour is to

make sure that you close every sale. Don't wait for the customer to do it.

STRESSED-OUT SALLY

A young salesperson related an interesting experience to me. A husband and wife had entered her store. She greeted them and asked if there was anything she could help them find. The woman said, "Paper clips. We need paper clips." The salesperson took her to the paper clips, but the wife said, "No, I need bigger ones." So the salesperson showed her the jumbo-sized paper clips, but the woman said, "No, I need some that are even bigger than that." The salesperson apologized, said that they didn't carry them in any larger size, but offered to see if they could be ordered.

Without any warning, the woman suddenly burst into tears and said, "Our house just burned down! It burned down to the ground. My cat died." The salesperson responded, "Oh, how awful," then waited a moment to see if there was any connection between this incident and the paper clips. Suddenly, the woman whirled on the salesperson, shoved her face two inches from the salesperson's face, and snarled, "I told you my cat died!" The woman and her husband then turned and walked out of the store.

Stress can do strange things to people. The greater the stress, the stranger people will behave. But unless the customer is under stress that you personally have created, there is little you can really do about it. And although she may be behaving oddly, your customer doesn't really expect you to do anything about it. She isn't really blaming you for her problems — she simply needed an outlet, and you happened to be handy.

The best response when this sort of thing happens is no response. You will only make matters worse.

Conclusion

Well, that about covers it. We've addressed most of our Customers from Hell, and even outlined some of the things to keep in mind so we don't become Salespeople from Hell. We've talked about unsatisfied customers, and about how you can use the principles of LESTER to win them over and turn them into loyal customers. We've talked about some broad categories of unreasonable customers, as well as some specific strategies for dealing with each type. We haven't covered them all, but let's face it — there are a lot of weird people out there. Even if you're armed with the best knowledge and are as prepared as you can be, chances are that sometime in your retail career you are going to be surprised by a customer with some new and inventive way to drive you nuts.

Retail is about people. Life is about people. And more often than not, the difference between our successes and our failures hinges on the strength of our communication skills. The wonderful thing about retail is that it gives us an opportunity to hone our communication skills every day. We learn how to develop relationships and how to make people feel good about themselves. We learn how to work with customers, peers, and superiors. We learn how much of an impact one person can have on the lives of others.

Dealing effectively with conflict and confrontation is both a communication skill and a lifestyle choice. When you're faced with conflict, you have only three choices: you can try to resolve it, you can try to win it, or you can try to run from it. This book has focused on the first option. Earlier on in the book, I asked, "Which is more important to you: winning a fight or ending a fight?" It's an important question, and you should be very frank with yourself in answering it, because the communication skills you require for each option are quite different.

I can promise you that mastering the skills for resolving conflict will serve you well throughout your life. As you perfect these skills, you will earn people's respect, trust, and confidence. I've never heard anyone say, "Geez, I hate that woman; she's always finding positive solutions to conflict." My guess is that if you had the patience to read this far into the book, then you are probably willing to practise the techniques I've outlined. If you do, you will find that there are fewer and fewer situations you can't handle. For those occasional ones that still stump you, remember these famous words from the days of vaudeville: Never let them see you sweat.